30 Days

to

Successful Fundraising

Dr. Stephen L. Goldstein

Grid Press® / PSI Research
Central Point, Oregon

Published by Grid Press®
© 2003 by Dr. Stephen L. Goldstein

This publication is designed to provide accurate and authoritative information in regard to the subject matter covered. It is sold with the understanding that the publisher is not engaged in rendering legal, accounting, or other professional service. If legal advice or other expert assistance is required, the services of a competent professional person should be sought.

> *— from a declaration of principles jointly adopted by a committee of the American Bar Association and a committee of publishers.*

Editor: Constance C. Dickinson
Assistant Editors: Harley Patrick and Jan Olsson
Book Designer: Constance C. Dickinson
Cover Designer: Mark Hannah

Please direct any comments, questions, or suggestions regarding this book to Grid Press®/PSI Research, Inc.:

Editorial Department
P.O. Box 3727
Central Point, OR 97502
(541) 245-6502
(541) 245-6505 *fax*
info@psi-research.com *e-mail*

Grid Press® is a Registered Trademark of Publishing Services, Inc., an Oregon corporation doing business as PSI Research, Inc.

Library of Congress Cataloging-in-Publication Data

Goldstein, Stephen L., 1943–
    30 days to successful fundraising / Stephen L. Goldstein.
        p. cm.
Includes index.
    ISBN 1-55571-636-9 (pbk.)
  1. Fund raising. I. Title: Thirty days to successful fundraising. II. Title.
    HG177.G654 2003
    658.15'224—dc22   2003020779

Printed in the United States of America
First edition 10 9 8 7 6 5 4 3 2 1

 Printed on recycled paper when available.

Contents

"Ask, and it shall be given to you; seek and ye shall find; knock, and it shall be opened unto you."

– Matthew VI:7

Your Path to Fundraising Success

There is no end of money to be had for worthwhile purposes. The challenge is simply to find the right match between donor and recipient. The best fundraising is the art of making that connection.

I developed this program because success eludes too many people. Most of us become fundraisers by default, not by design. We get a job—then discover that raising money is an important part of the responsibilities. Without formal training, confidence for doing the job can be elusive. Typically, learning on-the-job—picking up tips from here and there and attending a seminar now and again—makes it difficult to know when one has mastered the art.

For working people who need a quick, yet reliable, format in which to learn, *30 Days to Successful Fundraising* provides a practical, step-by-step method that enables anyone involved in fundraising—volunteers, people new to the field, even mature professionals—to build a solid foundation and master the basics. Go through the program from start to finish and you will increase both your fundraising ability and personal success.

The secret to successful fundraising is to know where the money is before you ask for it. In addition, you must learn to apply your time, energy, people skills, and resources to adequately cultivate your relationships with prospective funders.

Also important is developing good working relationships with your support team because they can play a significant role in your success, or failure. The process of cultivating successful relationships can take more time than you want or expect, which can be frustrating, but without this crucial activity neither you nor your fundraising efforts can succeed.

Fundraising is not a science. At a time when people are becoming increasingly dependent upon computers and other machines to do their work, it is crucial to remember that no amount of technology will ever be able to fundraise. It is a human process that takes place between people—people who want something and others who have something. When done successfully, it can be exhilarating and highly rewarding.

As you will see throughout this program, fundraising is not simply about asking for money. It is a mixture of psychology, marketing, common sense, good strategy, and a host of other sensitivities, the end result of which happens to be the acquisition of resources.

Learning good fundraising practices takes commitment. Don't be in a rush. Approach this 30 day program one Day, or chapter, at a time. Give yourself time to absorb, assess, and apply its messages. Avoid the temptation to sit down and read it from cover to cover. Instead, use the material deliberately to shape your fundraising plans and guide your professional thinking and activities.

The key to making a success of any program is to personalize its premises and principles, making them the basis of your constructive new habits and ways of thinking.

To that end, each Day in this book concludes with exercises titled "Applying This Principle to My Fundraising Success." The exercises are designed to allow you to tailor the principles covered to your particular fundraising project. By the time you finish this 30-day program, you will have a detailed, unique, and motivational road map for achieving your fundraising goals.

*"Nothing ever succeeds which
exuberant spirits have not helped
to produce."*

– Nietzsche

Find Your Burning Desire

You cannot succeed in life or in fundraising if you have an anemic goal, mission, or vision statement. You must be consumed by a "burning desire" to achieve something. Under those circumstances, you will succeed, even against what would appear to be insurmountable odds. If you do not have a burning desire, you may achieve some measure of success, but it will never be as great as it could have been had you been truly committed, even consumed, by your purpose.

Successful fundraising is not about asking for money. If fundraising were simply about asking for money, anybody would be able to do it, and everybody would be successful at it. It would be nothing more than a matter of saying, "Here I am. I represent a worthy cause. Please contribute to it." End of story.

As is usually the case, nothing is quite what it seems. Of course, the process of fundraising does involve asking for money or for other resources at some point. But successful fundraising involves much more than that. First, and most importantly, you must have a burning desire to change something in the world for the better. You have to identify an idea that will inspire, impress, excite, uplift, and encourage others to believe that they too can make a difference in the world by contributing to your project, your purpose, your burning desire. In addition, the most successful fundraising efforts are a mixture of the idealistic and uplifting with the practical and doable. They must have vision, promise, and scope; yet, they must appear to be accomplishable.

Thought rules the world. Everything and everyone in the world is driven by an idea. Thought sets everything in motion; and everyone has a good reason for what they do. Mother Teresa was almost consumed by her desire to care for the poorest of the poor. President John F. Kennedy energized the country when he embraced and pursued the idea of landing a man on the moon. Dr. Martin Luther King, Jr. inspired millions as he led the civil rights movement in the United States.

Such devotion to passion and principle is not, however, reserved only for the famous and powerful; it can motivate the behavior of most people. A grocer believes that if his store sells only organically grown foods it will help improve his customers' quality of life. The owner of a medical technology company develops noninvasive diagnostic and treatment procedures because she cares about her patients' well-being. A teacher discovers a better way to teach children to read.

Too often, in the process of anticipating the search for funds, fundraisers forget or take for granted the underlying idea that inspired their purpose or project, focusing only on the acquisition of dollars. Such an unworthy focus is almost certain to limit or destroy any otherwise worthy fundraising effort.

In fundraising, as in business, money follows great ideas. You must have or you must find a purpose that has heart and soul in it. You will know it when you see it and feel it. You will experience an "ah ha" about it. Others will too. You should be able to express your burning desire in one carefully crafted sentence; and, after hearing that sentence, others should be able immediately to grasp what you are trying to achieve.

Sometimes, an idea that started as a burning desire burns out over time and needs to be rekindled. Be flexible. Be willing to go back to basics. Where there is no heart, there will be no success. If you are starting a new project, be sure that you know and can fan the flames of your burning desire before you take a single step.

Resources

Harold J. Seymour, *Designs for Fund-Raising*, Second Edition. Fundraising Institute. Ambler, Pennsylvania, 1988.

The Foundation Center
79 Fifth Avenue
New York, NY 10003
(212) 620-4230
(212) 691-1828 (FAX)
(800) 424-9836 (customer service)
www.foundationcenter.org

The Foundation Center
1001 Connecticut Avenue, N.W., Suite 938
Washington, DC 20036
(202) 331-1400
(202) 331-1739 (FAX)
www.fdncenter.org/washington

The Foundation Center fosters public understanding of the foundation field by collecting, organizing, analyzing, and disseminating information on foundations, corporate giving, and related subjects.

Applying This Principle to My Fundraising Success

What do you feel is so important about your project?

_____

_____

_____

_____

_____

_____

_____

_____

_____

_____

_____

_____

_____

What single sentence sums it up?

_____

_____

_____

_____

_____

One hand cannot applaud alone.

– Ancient proverb

Keep Your Burning Desire from Going Up in Smoke

This is reality check time. Although extremely important, having a burning desire is only the initial element of the fundraising equation. Equally important is finding other people who will become as enthusiastic as you are about what you want to do; otherwise, you will get nowhere. Unless you are rigorously objective about the logic and value of what you want to do, your efforts to communicate will fall on deaf ears.

Only too often, people who set out to raise money end up being disappointed. They raise less than they set out to and not enough to accomplish their objectives, because they neglect putting themselves in the place of those who are in a position to help fund their project. They are so convinced what they are doing or want to do is so compelling, they think that others should support it on face value. They don't imagine how other people might react because they fail to assess objectively the real marketability of their ideas, so they operate in a vacuum.

Tunnel vision is a natural condition of experts in any field or of people who are closely involved in any project or effort. After a while, they cannot see the forest for the trees. But this limited view must be overcome. Ultimately, you must convince others to burn with the same desire about your project as you do—or you will have to foot the bill for funding it yourself.

The hardest thing to do is to think objectively and critically, beyond the limitations of your own knowledge and propensities, but that is the first exercise to which all successful fundraising projects must be subjected. In business it might be called a market analysis or a feasibility study. It is nothing more or less than checking the information available and testing the waters to see if your project makes enough sense and has enough potential payback to justify others investing in it.

The process of determining the marketability of a fundraising project is part art and part science. Before your proposal or concept is set in stone, you must spend time asking for the reactions and advice of people who are likely to be contributors. You must listen carefully with an open mind. Gather as much feedback as you can from your potential funders, so you can tackle your next step. If you can be objective and can keep your eye on the goal, the next step will be much less difficult.

Suppose, after doing a careful analysis, talking with enough people to get a feel for their reaction to helping you fund your project, you discover that your project is flawed—in potential funders' eyes. You face one of two important choices. You can go ahead with your project as it was originally conceived, convinced that you will eventually find more enlightened others who will support you. Or, you can decide to modify your proposal or even scrap the project or the proposal altogether. The choice is up to you.

One thing is clear, however. Your burning desire alone is not sufficient to ensure the success of your fundraising. At some point, your proposal must be able to stand on its own merits and convince complete strangers of your project's worth. Unless you are willing to be flexible and to adjust to external realities, you may see your burning desire go up in smoke.

Resource

Mimi Carlson, *Team-Based Fundraising Step-by-Step: A Practical Guide to Improving Results through Teamwork.* Jossey-Bass Publishers. San Francisco, California, 1997.

Applying This Principle to My Fundraising Success

Potential contributors who can help with a reality check.

What suggestions do they have?

What modifications might improve results?

"An intelligent plan is the first step to success.

The man who plans knows where he is going, knows what progress he is making and has a pretty good idea when he will arrive . . . .

If you don't know where you are going, how can you expect to get there?"

– Basil S. Walsh

Know the Fundraising Cycle

Successful fundraising is rarely a one-time affair. More often than not, it is a cyclical process that finds one campaign beginning where the last you left off. Along the way there are a number of crucial steps or stages you must consider. In fact, there are 12 such steps, with the final step preparing you for the next cycle.

It can be helpful to picture this 12-step fundraising cycle imposed on the face of a clock. If you were to begin the process at 12:00 noon, then the evolution of your plan would proceed as follows:

Research

Step 1 (12:00–1:00). Each time you set out to fundraise, begin by taking a look at what you have done in the past. Before you can determine where you want to go, you have to know where you are and where you have been. Obviously, you can't do this if it's your first time around, but you might be able to investigate the fundraising strategies and trends of a project similar to the one for which you plan to solicit funds. Capitalize on your experience and on the experience of others. You will save both time and money.

Step 2 (1:00–2:00). Regardless of whether your fundraising is under way or you are planning to begin a new venture, you should do as much market research as you can to determine what projects help the groups of people you serve or want to serve, as well as what potential donors want and feel they would support. During this phase of your research, you are simply trying to find out what are current concerns. Avoid preconceived notions and yesterday's truisms. Look for answers to the questions: What do people want and need today? and What will sell today and tomorrow?

Step 3 (2:00–3:00). Even if you already have a funded program or activity in place, you need to take a fresh look at it in light of what you learned in steps 1 and 2. You may want to modify your existing efforts or even propose new ones. Don't change for the sake of change, but always be alert to new possibilities.

Strategy

Step 4 (3:00–4:00). This is your moment of decision, the point at which you develop your strategy. You know the kind of program or activity you want to pursue—and the priorities of funders. Are they completely compatible? How flexible are you willing to be?

Step 5 (4:00–5:00). Develop your proposal. Depending upon your resources and your ability to change, you may or may not be able to make all of the modifications in existing programs that your research suggests might be needed—if it suggests any.

Step 6 (5:00–6:00). This stage is vital to your success. You know who your potential funders are and what you plan to propose to them. Now, you must ascertain how best to reach them with your message.

- Identify the people who can help you reach the people you need to help you—they are the linchpins of your success.
- Develop or obtain any collateral materials that will support your proposal.
- Be certain that the basics are taken care of—accurate street and e-mail addresses, phone and fax numbers.
- Plan your public relations strategy—the media outlets you will use to create awareness of your efforts.

Step 7 (6:00–7:00). Contact your network of linchpin individuals and determine those who are willing to support your efforts and exactly how they will assist you.

Implementation

Step 8 (7:00–8:00). Produce your proposal. Form should follow content. It can be as brief as one page or as elaborate as a printed brochure. Make it—including collateral material—appropriate to the scope of your project.

Step 9 (8:00–9:00). Put your complete plan into effect. Send your proposal to funders. Ask the people who support your efforts to help with solicitations. Release the publicity about your organization and your programs.

Evaluation

Step 10 (9:00–10:00). Collect data. Always learn from what you are doing as you are doing it. In this way, all of your historical or current efforts can help you in the future. For example, find out why potential funding prospects responded negatively to your solicitation. Keep track of the people who really did support your efforts and those who did not or could not in the end. Assess the giving levels of everyone. Could they have given you more now? Could they give you even more in the future?

Step 11 (10:00–11:00). Analyze your data. It isn't enough to collect information, you must use it to improve your chances for your future success. You must be able to recognize the strengths and weaknesses in your strategy that are revealed through analysis.

Step 12 (11:00–12:00). Write up your analysis, even if only you and a few others will see it. In the ongoing process of fundraising, the completion of one cycle becomes the foundation of the next cycle. Thus, you will use the data and information you have collected and the lessons you've learned along the way when your next fundraising process begins again at Step 1. So, the cycle is complete only when you are even better prepared to take on your next fundraising campaign.

Resource

The Support Center of Washington
2001 "O" Street, N.W.
Washington, DC 20036-5955
(202) 833-0300
(202) 857-0077 (FAX)
www.scw.org

Applying This Principle to My Fundraising Success

Research

Check other projects. _____

_____

_____

_____

What do people want/need? _____

_____

_____

_____

_____

What might improve results?

_____

_____

_____

_____

_____

Strategy

Choose your target(s).

_____

_____

_____

_____

Develop your proposal.

_____

_____

_____

_____

Obtain support materials and plan your PR.

_____

_____

_____

_____

Contact your network.

_____

_____

_____

_____

Implementation

Produce your proposal.
_____
_____
_____
_____

Put your plan in motion.
_____
_____
_____
_____

Evaluation

Keep track of how effective your plan is.
_____
_____
_____
_____

Analyze your findings.
_____
_____
_____
_____

Write up an analysis for future reference.
_____
_____
_____
_____
_____

"Words, words, words."

– *Hamlet*, II, ii, 195

Learn to Speak Fundraising

Every field of human endeavor develops its own special vocabulary, and fundraising is no exception. You need to become familiar with the words and phrases commonly used by fundraisers, because sometimes there are important legal distinctions and implications between various aspects of giving—such as restricted and unrestricted gifts.

Annual fund drive. Annual fund drives are the bread-and-butter of non-profits, the yearly solicitations for funds that provide their necessary ongoing funding. Annual fund drives are efforts to raise restricted as well as unrestricted gifts.

Capital campaign. Capital fund drives are the 500-pound gorillas of fundraising. They are major, multi-year, multi-million- or billion-dollar campaigns to raise money—primarily for buildings and endowment—that usually serve to bring an institution to a new level of philanthropic support and to expand the scope and quality of its programs and services.

Case statement. A publication that tells people why they should make a contribution to your project or organization and why you are the perfect organization to be trying to do what you propose. Among other things, it identifies the need(s) for which you are seeking funds, gives the history of your organization, and tells what programs or activities you plan to develop and for which you need funding.

Corporate giving program. Unlike a foundation—a separate corporate entity into which monies are placed for charitable purposes—a corporation's giving program is usually an amount set aside annually for philanthropic purposes.

Deferred gift. Most people who are seeking funds focus on their organizations current need(s) and on soliciting immediate contributions. But sometimes, the largest gifts may be obtained as deferred gifts, given upon a donor's death, for example. Focus on both short- and long-term fundraising, and find creative ways to enable contributors to support your efforts.

Donative intent (see Restricted gift). For donors, the reason they give money is more important than the donation itself. For example, you may be a college or university soliciting funds for a variety of reasons, but a given donor may want a contribution given for a specific purpose—like scholarships—but for no other purpose. As the recipient of those funds, you must respect the wishes of the donor, the donative intent, and not use the contribution other than to honor the donor's original purpose.

501(c). The United States Internal Revenue Service code recognizes charitable organizations—those that may receive tax-deductible contributions—under its 501(c) subsections. Unless an organization is officially designated in this way, donors to it cannot receive a tax break.

Foundation. A formal, non-profit corporate entity that makes contributions for charitable purposes. Some foundations give large amounts of money away; others have only limited resources.

Perhaps, the best known foundations are those that have been established by major corporations or wealthy individuals, such as the Ford Foundation. Funds contributed to a 501(c) designated U.S. foundation are tax deductible. Usually, foundations establish priorities for giving; for example, health care, education, the homeless. Each foundation has its own guidelines for requesting money. No two foundations are alike. Unless the foundation is small, expect to jump through many hoops to get funding.

Fundraising pyramid. You have to set your sights on large gifts if you're going to be successful. Knowing that, professional fundraisers usually think in terms of a pyramid when they map out a campaign, recognizing that not everyone will be willing or able to contribute the same amount of money. They indicate how many large gifts will be needed at the top and how many smaller donations at the bottom.

Gift-in-kind. Valuable contributions don't always come in the form of money; they may be products or services that, of course, have a dollar value. Rather than donating money to a school, a manufacturer of computers may choose to contribute actual computers, thereby offsetting what would otherwise be a cost to the educational institution. Only accept truly useful items as gifts-in-kind; otherwise, your organization will wind up with a lot of other people's tax deductions that are of little or no value to you.

Lead gift. In fundraising, as in life, monkey-see is monkey-do. Credibility and momentum come to campaigns when someone steps forward with a major, or lead, gift. In a campaign to raise $1 million, for example, the person who starts the ball rolling with a $500,000 contribution will inspire others to contribute at perhaps lesser, but equally important, levels.

Recognition ladder. Too often, people emphasize the importance of asking for charitable gifts, but neglect to recognize or thank people. You should have a clear description of how donors of the smallest to the largest amounts will be acknowledged—before you set out to raise your first dollar.

Restricted gift (see Donative intent). Sometimes donors attach specific restrictions to their gifts. For example, they may want their funds used only for capital or building projects; they may indicate that they do not want their donation to be used for endowment; or they may stipulate that their contribution be earmarked for medical research, not clinical services. These donor preferences must be honored to the letter.

Unrestricted gift. A donation that has no strings attached to it is considered "unrestricted," to be used at your discretion to advance the goals and purposes of your project and organization. Even so, you must still use it for a purpose consistent with your project's stated intent.

Resource

The Grantsmanship Center
1125 W. 6th Street
Los Angeles, California
(213) 482-9860
(213) 482-9863 (FAX)

The center provides training programs, conducts workshops, has a research staff, and publishes resource materials.

Applying This Principle to My Fundraising Success

Memorize one fundraising term each day for the next 14 days.

_____

_____

_____

_____

_____

_____

_____

He who allows his day to pass by without practicing
generosity and enjoying life's pleasures is like a
blacksmith's bellows—he breathes
but does not live.

– Sanskrit Proverb

Create a Winning Budget

The best way to define, then refine, your fundraising objectives is to develop your budgetary requirements. There comes a time when every burning desire has to be subjected to a reality check—and that usually means establishing the amount of money it will realistically take to accomplish your goals.

Funding sources do not respond well to vagueness; they want clear budgets, timelines, and outcomes. Donors want to know exactly to what effort and resources they are being asked to contribute. For them, your proposed project is a risk and an investment. They want as much certainty in its positive outcome as possible. That certainty will come from the combination of a perceivably worthwhile aim and responsible financial projections.

Obviously, your budget has to be complete and make fiscal sense, but don't limit your presentation just to the numbers. Use your budget to make the case for your project in "dollars-and-sense" terms. For example, make interpretative statements at strategic points about the cost-effectiveness of your proposal. Guide potential funders through your budget strategically.

Follow these 10 basic guidelines while developing your budget:

1. Do not pad your proposal budget with more money than you really need, anticipating that you will have a chance later to negotiate it to a more realistic figure. You probably will not be given that chance because your proposal will be rejected out-of-hand. Funders do not play games or like game-players.

2. Consider developing two or three different budget scenarios, based upon projects of varying scope depending upon funding, with each able to stand on its own.

3. Stress the dollars you have and are willing to spend. Always include the indirect dollar values your organization is contributing to a project—the allocation of staff and in-kind services, for example—and other ways you support it.

4. Demonstrate the cost-effectiveness of the way you and your organization conduct business. Use comparative data to show how your costs are in line with or more economical than those of comparable entities.

5. Where appropriate, indicate that you can produce a cost-effective result. For example, if you are providing clinical services or educational programs, show how you can do it better and for less money than anyone else does.

6. Resist the human tendency to ignore certain inevitable, unanticipatable costs and to think that they will somehow take care of themselves. Instead, budget a specific lump sum for the unexpected.

7. Include dollars for the dissemination of information about your project. Describe how the positive press you generate will help you to attract additional donations.

8. Emphasize how you can save and stretch dollars contributed through collaborative efforts with other appropriate individuals and agencies.

9. Budget for your increasing self-sufficiency and, ideally, financial independence. Funders do not want to see a budget that will obligate them forever or that will rely solely upon the largess of others. Demonstrate how your project will be able to become less dependent on contributed monies as time goes on.

10. Budget for start-up costs and for the dollars associated with responsibly closing out a project, should that be necessary.

A well-designed, illuminating budget proposal is a persuasive fundraising tool.

Resource

National Directory of Corporate Giving
The Foundation Center
79 Fifth Avenue
New York, NY 10003
(212) 620-4230
(212) 691-1828 (FAX)
(800) 424-9836

Applying This Principle to My Fundraising Success

Develop two or three different budget scenarios for the same (real or hypothetical) project.

_____

_____

_____

_____

_____

_____

Write a brief narrative comparing the scope and outcomes of each budget scenario.

_____

_____

_____

_____

_____

_____

_____

_____

_____

_____

_____

_____

_____

_____

_____

_____

_____

_____

_____

_____

_____

_____

_____

_____

_____

_____

_____

_____

_____

"Angels rush in where fools fear to tread."

– Author

Get the Money Wherever You Can Find It

There are really only three ways to raise money. Master them and you'll be able to fund every project you undertake.

First, Go Where the Money Is

Some fundraising consultants advise their clients to go after only big gifts, right from the start, and ignore smaller contributors. They contend that more is always better in fundraising; the bigger the gift(s) you receive, the sooner you will reach your fundraising goals, the more successful your project is likely to be, and the easier your life will probably be. They pursue only the most likely sources of major funding and argue against wasting your time on a larger number of smaller gifts. They point out that it takes less time to ask for one gift of $50,000 than it does to ask for 50 of $1,000.

That advice would be plausible were it not unrealistic. People with access to large sums of money are not sitting around waiting for you to approach them. And once approached, even if they can afford to donate substantial moneys to you, they may take a wait-and-see approach. You must cultivate major donors; they don't automatically spring into action on behalf of you, your organization, or your project.

Ultimately, your realistic strategy should not be either-or, either big gifts or small gifts, but all gifts—big and small and everything in between. You must develop an approach that will enable you to identify likely sources of major funding, as well as worthwhile prospects for lesser gifts.

Eventually, contributors of lesser gifts may give substantially more than you ever imagined they would or could. Wisely, someone once said that in fundraising you don't have to find the people who *have* the largest amount of money, but the people who are willing to *give* the largest amount of money.

Second, Get the Money to Come to You

In addition to specifically identifying potential funding sources (individuals, foundations, corporations, government agencies, etc.), you need to make your search for funding known to the widest possible audiences. Get the word out in every way possible. For example, arrange to speak before groups that might be sympathetic to your goals.

Eventually, as a result of your publicizing your project and fundraising needs, someone somewhere will tell someone else about your project that will lead to a direct contribution.

Third, Smoke Out the Money

Young and old, everyone loves to play games. We all want to take sides and be on the winning team. One way to generate donations in short order is to create a Challenge Game. By doing so, you may be able to double or even triple the dollars you can raise.

Here's how the game works. Find a person or persons willing to donate a substantial amount of money—if, and only if, their contribution is matched 1 to 1, 2 to 1, or according to some other ratio, by a certain date. In other words, your $100,000 donor comes forward and presents a challenge to others, "Match my gift 2 to 1 within a year—or lose my $100,000."

Now you can go armed with the best reasons for someone to make a donation to your project: "Any amount you give will be doubled" and "Please don't let us lose this generous gift and the money that will match it." Through challenges, large and small gifts come together. Everyone in your donor base can participate and feel that they are giving more than they would otherwise.

If you plan your challenge properly, knowing in advance that you can meet it and where the money will come from, you can create great excitement and a feeling of genuine accomplishment—and, possibly, even exceed your expectations. If you meet your challenge before your time is up, don't stop. The challenge is for a specified period of time, as well as for a certain amount of money. There is nothing wrong with doing better than anyone thought you could. That's the best part of the game.

Resource

Philanthropy News Digest
www.fdncenter.org/pnd/

News, job information, reports on foundations, and grants—a wealth of information online from The Foundation Center.

Applying This Principle to My Fundraising Success

List five likely sources of funding for your organization.

_____

_____

_____

_____

_____

_____

Identify five groups you could speak before about your project.

_____

_____

_____

_____

_____

_____

List two or three people you might approach for a challenge grant.

_____

_____

_____

_____

_____

_____

"[Unless a person] is able to sell himself and his ideas, unless he has the power to convince others of the soundness of his conclusions, he can never achieve his goal."

– Robert E. M. Cowie

Sell Ideas that Sell

The most successful fundraising begins and ends with an idea that sells. Yet, even though a worthwhile project or idea that you have may appeal to you and be justified on any number of levels, it may not resonate with people who are potential funders. Still, as long as you need to fundraise for a project, you must find ways to make it appealing—to make it sell—to attract money.

Such a realization may come as a shock, particularly to those who believe strongly in the legitimacy of their activities and who shy away from what might appear to be pandering to public taste just to raise a buck. But the truth of the matter is that fundraising is a two-sided equation. And both sides are equally important. You cannot expect anyone to support your efforts unless you meet them half way. Others must see and feel value in what you are doing. You must prove to them that there is inherent value in your project. The mere fact that you are a expert in a field or that you see the importance of a project does not ensure its automatic success.

In advertising, professionals say, "Sell the sizzle, not the steak." In other words, it is the underlying, rather than the overt, motivation that attracts people's attention. You don't show an unappealing piece of raw beef on a plate in an ad and expect people to flock to your restaurant. You show it succulently cooked, surrounded by irresistible garnishings, displayed on a complementary plate in an impeccable table setting, and desired by an attractive couple dining in an exclusive and elegant setting. The recipe for success: you are selling romance and sophistication—the sizzle, not the beef.

It is the same in fundraising. You need to surround your proposal with all of the sizzle about what your project can do for the world-at-large. Cast your project in a light that makes the benefits abundantly clear, allowing potential donors to visualize the advantages of their involvement.

Fortunately, compelling pitches are everywhere to be found. The way to give your worthy proposal the boost it needs—to become a compelling reason for people to give money to support it—is to relate it to a compelling trend that is shaping the future of our world. It cannot be something that is simply new and different, a mere fad. It must be something that is important to society—to large numbers of otherwise advantaged or disadvantaged people—and something that puts you in a leadership position.

> Example 1. Increasingly during the coming decades, water shortages will cause untold hardship, disease, and death to innocent people around the globe. A revolutionary technique to desalinate ocean water or other means of increasing the earth's potable water supply would be likely to attract the attention and funding of major donors.

> Example 2. Illiteracy is a persistent and growing problem worldwide. For all of the good intentions that have gone into trying to increase literacy, nothing seems to have

made a major difference. If you find whatever you believe to be the way to make things better and present your solution in a compelling way, you may attract substantial funding from a wide range of funding sources.

The burden of framing and substantiating the trend you chose is obviously yours. You must find hard data from impeccable sources to create a context for your proposal.

In addition, fundraising ideas that sell best are results-oriented. You must make the case for funding your proposal by including projections about the difference that your project can make in stemming or reversing a negative trend or in advancing a positive one. Funders want (and deserve) to feel that they are investing in something that will pay off and about which they can feel good.

Resource

Alliance for Nonprofit Management
1899 L Street, N.W., Suite 600
Washington, DC 20036
www.allianceonline.org/

Association of individuals and organizations devoted to improving the management and governance capacity of nonprofits and assisting nonprofits in fulfilling their mission. Its Web site is a wealth of information on everything from careers to board development.

Applying This Principle to My Fundraising Success

Identify the major trend to which your fundraising proposal relates.

_____

_____

_____

_____

Provide key data to elaborate on the urgency and importance of your helping to stop a bad trend or advance a good one.

_____

_____

_____

_____

_____

_____

_____

_____

_____

_____

_____

_____

_____

List three to five "sizzles" that would sell a potential donor on contributing to your project.

_____

_____

_____

_____

_____

_____

_____

"When you cannot make up your mind which of two evenly balanced courses of action you should take, choose the bolder."

– W. J. Slim

Apply the Law of Completion

The little-known "law of completion" may be the most powerful piece of information in your arsenal of successful fundraising strategies. Pay particular attention to the nuances that it reveals about every donor—actual or potential.

No matter how reasonable your proposal for funds may be or how rational you are in making the case for giving to support your effort, never lose sight of the fact that a determining factor in successful fundraising is emotion or irrationality. Ultimately, people give not because you have convinced them to but because you have awakened an emotional connection to something about which they feel strongly.

You can have all the facts and figures you need and the most convincing of arguments, but unless you touch upon the deep seeded motivators—the emotional well-spring—of your potential donors, you will never reach them with your message.

Despite the defenses of sophistication, skepticism, and hesitancy, deep down everyone wants to make a positive difference in the world. At the broadest level, they want to see physical suffering mitigated, poverty reduced or eliminated, illiteracy overcome; in short, they want the world to be a place in which the lives of people of all ages can be fulfilling. This macro-emotional appeal may move them; however, it is not the most important or motivating part of a person's emotional make-up.

The micro-emotional level is where passion originates. Everyone on planet earth has some positive or negative, incomplete or unfulfilled experience in their personal history that motivates them to act. For example, a young man who suffered from polio in his youth becomes obsessed with physical achievement in order to compensate for it and becomes an Olympic gold medalist. An illiterate parent works as a maid so she can educate her children, and they can enjoy a better life. The ugly duckling, wallflower, or female nerd in high school becomes Miss America. Some people spend their lives trying to become what they think and feel they are not, and others want to abate some type of suffering.

As you might suspect, the law of completion not only applies in fundraising, it rules. People give to compensate for what they feel is incomplete in their lives. The successful entrepreneur who could not go to college because he couldn't afford to may be just the person to donate money to provide scholarships for needy students. A woman who was not able to bear children of her own may be the perfect donor to contribute to adoption or fertility programs. Having unexpectedly lost a daughter who was a teacher, a husband and wife might find comfort from contributing a fellowship in her name to memorialize her and help perpetuate her professional efforts.

Ignore the hot-button issues at your own peril. They are truly the ones that will open philanthropic doors and pockets for you. Of course, one reason people give money is because they can save money on taxes. But ultimately, people give money so they will feel better about themselves and about the world in which they live. Set out to reach them at their emotional, as well as their rational, level.

Resources

The Chronicle of Philanthropy
1255 Twenty-Third Street, N.W.
Washington, DC 20037
(202) 466-1200
http://philanthropy.com

The newspaper of the nonprofit world.

DM News
100 Avenue of the Americas
New York, NY 10013
(212) 925-7300
www.dmnews.com

The online newspaper of record for direct marketers.

Applying This Principle to My Fundraising Success

List five potential donors and their hot-button issues, the ones you can help them "complete" by supporting your cause.

_____

_____

_____

_____

_____

_____

"Fools rush in where angels fear to tread."

– Alexander Pope

Overcome Your Fear of Asking for Money

Deep down, at some level, everyone hesitates to ask for money, even if it is for a good cause. No matter how experienced we may be at fundraising, we all have a dollar threshold beyond which we are reluctant to go. Yet, unless we break through that psychological barrier, we will wind up being our own worst enemy, standing in the way of our greatest fundraising success. One surefire way to embolden yourself to ask for money of any amount is to remember that you are not asking for money for yourself, but to advance some worthy cause.

With that in mind, there is a right way to ask for money—and a wrong way. Much of the time, people ask the wrong way. Follow these guidelines to ask for money the right way.

↪ Initiate every funding request with a letter, followed up by a phone call. The one exception to this approach is in the strategy for soliciting major gifts (see Day 15).

It is bad strategy to place a cold call to anyone. Even if you do get through to them, your call will catch them off guard. They are only going to ask for follow-up information anyway. So, it is better to write beforehand and pave the way.

↪ Show that you know to whom you are writing or speaking.

Get to know the people you are soliciting before you ever meet them, but don't be so obvious as to let them know you have researched them, by dropping hints of the details of their life, for example. Some people might be flattered or impressed when you show them you've taken the time to find out about them before approaching them, but most will feel vulnerable, as though they are being treated like laboratory specimens. Behave as naturally toward them as you would toward friends and family, people whose reactions you can predict because you really know them.

Most large donors you will want to approach will have giving histories. From published and unpublished sources you should be able to determine their priorities. Let them know why you think that your project would be consistent with their interests.

↪ Personalize your communications.

Never write anything that could be construed as boiler plate to a potential donor, no matter how small the prospective gift. Even in a mass mailing, include some form of meaningful personalized message. Handwrite as many personal notes as you can, such as a P.S. on a mass mailing. If you can't do it all yourself, get a group of volunteers to do 100 personal notes each. You'll be amazed at the positive responses you'll get. Do anything to break the mold to communicate one-on-one.

↪ Be clear, straightforward, and precise.

Don't waste people's time. Grab their attention. State your request for funding in simple language that is easy to understand. Let them know exactly what you want from them.

↠ Ask for a specific amount or commitment.

Always include a specific call to action in your letter. Don't leave the ball in your donors' court; otherwise, they may simply choose to drop it.

↠ Be prepared with alternative scenarios.

Give your potential donors choices. For example, ask them to make an outright gift of $1,000 today or a gift of $500 this year and next. No one wants to feel as though they just knuckled under to you. They want to feel as though they made a decision. Set up your communications to enable them to take responsibility for their decisions.

↠ Make it easy for anyone to say, yes.

Of course, you may not win them all, but then again you might. Make your appeal so irresistible and flexible, that no one can refuse to give you something—even a small amount.

↠ It's okay to ask again, even after being rebuffed.

It isn't over until it's really over. Persistence is the key to success. Just because someone said no during one solicitation cycle doesn't mean they won't respond positively at another time. You may simply have caught them at a time when their funds were already committed. Unless they have positively told you that they would never be interested in a certain project for which you are still requesting funds, don't give up. Make a polite re-ask. After all, they know you better now.

↠ Ask for advice and assistance, especially from people you ask for money.

Ask everyone you solicit—even people who turn you down—for the names of others who, they think, might be interested in supporting your project. Such information can easily be as valuable as a financial contribution—perhaps even more so.

Think like a contributor. Ask for money the way you would want to be asked. Applying the golden rule is particularly appropriate in the field of fundraising.

Resource

Joan Flanagan, *Successful Fundraising: A Complete Handbook for Volunteers and Professionals.* Contemporary Books. Lincolnwood (Chicago), Illinois, 2000.

Applying This Principle to My Fundraising Success

List five ways you can personalize your communication with potential donors.

_____

_____

_____

_____

_____

_____

_____

_____

_____

_____

_____

_____

_____

_____

_____

_____

_____

_____

_____

_____

"All the world is a store, and all the people in it are salespeople. That is to say, every one of us human beings is trying to transfer an idea from his own head into some other brain. And that is the essence of salesmanship."

– Arthur Brisbane

Shape Your Ideas into Words and Visuals that Raise Money

Compelling language can translate into successful fundraising. There are no magical fundraising words, of course—words that in and of themselves can guarantee that people will donate to your cause. But there are ways to speak and write that will enhance your ability to get people's attention, so that you have a chance to convince them of the value of your project.

→ Use startling phrases or facts.

You need to look for an "ah-ha"—the kind of brief, arresting bit of information that startles you into achieving some realization that changes your attitude or perception. It is important to remember that your burning desire should change the way people look at the world and how they see themselves.

39

→ Use strong verbs.

Verbs are the most powerful words in any language; they fuel the momentum of your ideas. For example, instead of the verb "run," consider using "sprint." Instead of "break," substitute "shatter." Instead of "ate," try "devoured." Look for verbs packed with the kind of energy that will grab people's attention and move them emotionally. Study newspaper headlines and magazine covers for pithy, direct verbs.

→ Don't use flowery adjectives.

Some people seem to think that by embellishing otherwise bland statements with a sea of adjectives they can increase the significance and appeal of their ideas. Instead, they just turn others off by sounding undereducated or unsure of themselves.

→ Keep sentences short and to the point.

→ Use emotional, rather than rational, language.

→ Use a person-to-person tone, addressing your potential donors as though you were speaking with them one-on-one.

→ Always include a powerful visual to accompany the explanation of your project.

Ideally, it should be a compelling and professional looking photograph. A picture may be worth $10,000 to you, but it has to be clear and startling. Always include a caption with your picture or you will be destroying its potential punch. A visual without a caption is like a ship without a rudder. Your readers will not know how to interpret its significance unless you tell them what it is. Graphs and sketches may be acceptable to reinforce certain kinds of statements (comparative and performance figures, architect's renderings), but nothing is more compelling than a powerful photograph—except, perhaps, a dramatic video.

→ Repeat your message three times in different words.

The trick in repeating your message is not to appear redundant. You need to provide variations on your theme that will reinforce your message and pique your listeners' or readers' interest.

→ Include legitimate celebrity or expert endorsements, but only when they truly understand and support your efforts.

You may discover among the people associated with your organization that someone has a connection with a celebrity and is willing to ask him or her to become identified with your cause. However, proceed with caution if you want to ask for anyone's help or publicly promote an individual's working on your behalf. Audrey Hepburn's speaking on behalf of UNICEF was a fundraiser's dream come true, but she was a rare and special case. In general, the indisputable power of a celebrity endorsement can greatly help your fundraising efforts, but it can be a two-edged sword. Every well-known person has detractors as well as admirers. You must be careful whom you enlist as a spokesperson for your efforts. Flee from anyone who asks for a fee.

Craft compelling communications to your potential funding sources, and you'll be amazed at how successful your fundraising will be.

Resources

NonProfit Times
240 Cedar Knolls Road, Suite 318
Cedar Knolls, NJ 07927
(201) 734-1700
www.nptimes.com/

The leading business publication for nonprofit management.

Susan L. Golden, *Secrets of Successful Grantsmanship: A Guerrilla Guide to Raising Money.* Jossey-Bass Publishers. San Francisco, California, 1997.

Applying This Principle to My Fundraising Success

Write three sentences that give potential donors a different reason to contribute to your organization.

_____

_____

_____

_____

_____

_____

_____

Write a brief description of three different visuals you could use (photos, graphs, sketches) to enhance the impact of your three sentences.

_____

_____

_____

_____

_____

_____

_____

_____

_____

_____

_____

_____

_____

_____

". . . the credit goes to the man who convinces the world."

– Sir William Osler

Develop Your Case Statement

A case statement is a publication that provides pertinent information about your project. Every fundraising project, no matter how big or small, needs one. It should be a well-written piece that succinctly says everything you need to say about your program and organization. It serves the important purpose of telling potential donors everything they need to know about why your effort is worthy of receiving contributions. Even if you apply for funding from an organization or agency that has its own application form or format to follow, you should include your case statement as an additional information piece.

Your case statement doesn't have to be expensive or ambitious. It should look professional, however, even if it is nothing more than a typewritten publication. Wherever possible, try to use visuals and graphics to increase the power of your message.

It is a given that no two case statements should look exactly alike; after all, no two institutions or projects are identical. But here are seven basic elements you should include in your case statement.

1. Focus on critical trends in the introduction of your case statement.

   Establish the need for your proposed project by identifying the key trends it addresses. For example, if you are building a case for raising funds for a university so that it can deliver state-of-the-art educational programs through an array of emerging technologies, document the trends in "universities-without-walls" and in the needs and demands of the college students of the future as well as the corporations that will employ them.

2. State the goals and objectives of your project.

   Position your proposal as the most logical response to the challenges and opportunities created by the major trends you have identified. Excite the readers of your goals and objectives with the prospect of making a real difference in the lives of people by supporting you.

3. Qualify your organization.

   Demonstrate why your organization and its staff are uniquely positioned to undertake the project or program you propose. Document your track record with similar successful ventures. If you don't have a track record, show why you are best qualified and why donors should entrust their money to you. Include testimonial statements from respected individuals to bolster your case.

4. Include your budget.

   Avoid presenting your budget as a dry rehearsal of dollars and numbers. Insert brief narratives and interpretative statements at key points, engaging and guiding your readers through the intricacies of the budget.

5. Explain the benefits to potential contributors, whether they are individuals, corporations, foundations, or other entities.

Few individuals or organizations give selflessly; they want to receive something for their contribution. Include a range of benefits—from the tangible to the intangible—that will encourage people to donate to you. Indicate how donors will be recognized and how the goals will be met. Donors share with your organization the successes of the program(s) they help fund. Point out how corporate giving objectives can be met, including the positive publicity they will receive, by supporting your cause.

6. List the staff of your organization and their credentials.

   Make these biographies interesting and lively narratives that include only relevant information, not boring, pro forma resumes. Make people want to read about your superbly qualified and enthusiastic staff, board, researchers, professors, and doctors.

7. Include any legal documentation, indicating the non-profit status of your organization.

   You may not be able to do much to enliven this section of your case statement. But even here, do your best to make your material interesting. Don't take the path of least resistance.

Your case statement is your calling card, your letter of introduction, your door-opener. It can only sell your organization's message and purpose if you add to it your enthusiasm and commitment.

Resources

Mal Warwick, *How to Write Successful Fundraising Letters.* [eBook] Jossey-Bass. San Francisco, California, 2001.

Judith E. Nichols, *Transforming Fundraising: A Practical Guide to Evaluating and Strengthening Fundraising to Grow with Change.* Jossey-Bass Publishers. San Francisco, California, 1999.

Applying This Principle to My Fundraising Success

Draft a hypothetical mini-case statement. Write two sentences for each of the seven items that should be in your case statement.

_____

_____

_____

_____

_____

_____

_____

_____

_____

_____

_____

_____

_____

_____

_____

_____

_____

_____

_____

_____

_____

_____

_____

_____

_____

_____

_____

_____

_____

*"I could never divide myself from any man upon the
difference of an opinion."*

– Sir Thomas Browne

Apply Different Strokes for Different Folks

The age of mass-marketing and mass-communications is over, and
the era of micro-marketing has begun. The new realities of the
marketplace put increasing pressure on any organization that ad-
vertises its goods and services to particularize its message for numerous potential constituencies.

As frustrating as this may seem, there is no such thing as a single
piece of written material or sales pitch that will convince everyone
to contribute to your effort. As a result you must keep in mind several diverse interests as you prepare your communications.

→ Everything you produce to state the case for your fundraising
must be targeted as much as possible to a specific audience or

individual. You must learn to micro-market all of your communications, personalizing them as much as possible to each potential audience that you wish to reach.

→ Identify all of the target individuals and audiences from whom you might want to solicit funds.

→ Construct an appropriate micro-message for each group. Effective written materials will produce results only if you micro-communicate what people want to hear, as long as it is consistent with the purposes of your project.

→ The hardest thing to break through is a mind that is intent upon saying, "No." Learn to walk away from prospects who are immediately negative toward your project. Save them for another time—perhaps, after you are successful and have made a name for yourself. Then they may be more comfortable about jumping on board and supporting you. Write for open-minded audiences, people who can be persuaded to support you.

→ General campaign materials need to be broadly written.

→ Maintain the utmost flexibility in all of your printed materials, so you can tailor them to different audiences in a cost-effective manner.

→ Individual solicitations need to be painstakingly tailored for each person or organization that may give you major funds.

→ A picture may be worth $10,000 if it is the right picture. You will need to show different visuals to different people.

→ Unless you know someone who can arrange a face-to-face meeting, you have about 30 seconds to get the attention of foundations. Their staff are skeptical and busy, often indifferent. They think that they have heard almost everything before, and they probably have.

→ Unless you have a contact inside a company, solicit corporations as though they were preoccupied, condescending, and difficult. They are.

→ Unless you are contacting a friend or the friend of someone you know, when trying to reach individuals, bear in mind they are being approached by numerous other charity fundraisers, all of whom believe their cause is at least as worthy as yours.

Remember there are lions at everyone's gate—secretaries, assistants, family members—to protect them from the assaults of salespeople and charitable solicitations. The best way to get your case heard within a foundation or corporation, or by an individual, is to know someone on the board or among its executives, or within a person's circle of friends. Use your connections, your network of supporters, to open doors for you; otherwise, you'll be left out in the cold.

Resources

Fund$Raiser Cyberzine
www.fundsraiser.com

An online magazine dedicated to bringing fundraisers the latest and most complete news and ideas in fundraising.

Mal Warick, *The Five Strategies for Fundraising Success: A Mission Guide to Achieving Your Goals.* Jossey-Bass. San Francisco, California, 2000.

Applying This Principle to My Fundraising Success

In one sentence, write a general message about your fund raising.

_____

_____

_____

_____

_____

_____

Recast your general message with a specific focus to appeal to at least three different potential donor groups.

_____

_____

_____

_____

_____

_____

_____

_____

_____

_____

_____

_____

_____

_____

_____

_____

_____

_____

_____

_____

_____

_____

_____

_____

_____

_____

_____

"Ideas are the mightiest influence on earth. One great thought breathed into a man may regenerate him."

– Channing

Write a Compelling Sales Letter to Solicit Funds

To get the dollars that you need, you must inspire people with the worthiness of your cause or project. Money, as the saying goes, follows great ideas. Think of your activity on the highest plane. Use words and phrases that elevate without being flowery, that create enthusiasm, that inspire confidence, and that motivate people to contribute to your cause.

When you approach writing a letter to raise funds or ask for money, emphasize the values and objectives of, and need for, your organization. Focusing on the money as the objective can be the kiss of death in fundraising, as with other endeavors; and you will never be successful. This is especially true when going after major donations. (See Day 15.)

The best fundraising letters are sales letters that state compelling reasons why someone should support your cause.

→ Be absolutely certain to send your letter to the right person.

As obvious and simple as this might sound, you cannot imagine how many opening salvos in fundraising go sour because people do not take the time to find out to whom they should be writing. Even if you think you know, be absolutely sure before you send your letter. Reconfirm the person's title and address. There is nothing permanent; everything can change— and usually does. People don't like to see their name misspelled or to have an incorrect title assigned to them. You certainly don't want to be rejected at the start because of some obvious failure to check an error. Check and re-check to be certain your communication is accurate and headed in the right direction.

→ Let the recipient of the letter know right off that this is a solicitation for important funding for a significant project.

Don't spend a paragraph or two setting up your letter with a lot of dead-end rhetoric, then go in for the fundraising pitch. This transparent approach is a time-waster that irritates people.

→ Be merciful. Be brief.

Contributors are bombarded with appeals of every kind. Go easy on them. Get to the heart of the matter quickly. They will think well of you for not wasting their time.

→ Use an anecdote or example to humanize the issue or circumstance you are addressing in your proposal.

Everybody wants to hear a compelling story. Don't rely on just numbers and theoretical language to get your points across. Instead, use the power of a human interest anecdote to reinforce your reasons for giving.

→ Show how you are trying to help people, rather than talk about what you need.

Avoid the "we-we-we" approach. Make your communications outer-directed, not self-serving. No one is really interested in

what you need. They want to know what you are going to accomplish with the gift you may receive from them. They want
to know how you are going to help enhance the lives of others.

→ Use facts and data, not meaningless adjectives, to sell the value
of your proposal.

The facts and figures that state your case are unique to your
project. Adjectives can apply to anybody or anything. Businesspeople, especially, are swayed by the credibility implied in
numbers. Use concrete information to your advantage. Demonstrate that you, a non-profit, can act in a businesslike way.

→ Always end your letter with a P.S. that asks your potential
donor to make a contribution—today.

Plan to send a regular series of fundraising letters throughout the
year. Be sure to report on the success of previous letters (dollars
raised and good that was accomplished) because of the donations
you received.

Resource

Terry and Doug Schaff, *The Fundraising Planner: A Working
Model for Raising the Dollars You Need.* Jossey-Bass Publishers.
San Francisco, California, 1999.

Applying This Principle to My Fundraising Success

Verify the contact information for at least five potential donors.

_____

_____

_____

_____

_____

_____

Write the first paragraph of a hypothetical fundraising letter.

_____

_____

_____

_____

_____

_____

_____

_____

_____

_____

_____

_____

_____

_____

_____

Write a snappy P.S. that prompts a potential contributor to donate.

_____

_____

_____

_____

_____

_____

_____

_____

_____

"Never be involved in a cause that has a weak leader."

– Unknown

Find Your Leaders and Establish Your Personal Network

"People give to people" is a truism in fundraising. The right people asking people they know to give to a cause with which they identify can assure the success of almost any project. Your challenge is to find a core group of influential people and convince them to support you, then to motivate them to get others to support you.

Ideally, all the members of your board will provide the fundraising leadership you need—giving money and encouraging others to give as well. Realistically, you will be lucky if you can recruit or energize even a few vigorous board members. Even so, make it your goal to inspire as many of your board members as possible to become solid givers.

Most of all, you need leaders among leaders, people who will step forward and take a major role in soliciting others to give serious money on your behalf. Many people can help you out by donating their own resources; few will actually step forward and work for you. But it only takes one or two committed and well-connected people to make the difference between a struggling and a wildly successful fundraising effort.

This principle of leadership identification applies whether you are raising funds for a small project or an extensive, multi-million-dollar campaign. You must always work through community leaders to establish your support base.

Some people are naturals at opening doors. They are able to get through to others. But, in addition, you need individuals who are sufficiently committed to your efforts to make a large donation, then help you raise other significant funds. Only those who have given money themselves can help you ask someone else for money; and, legitimately, they can only ask others to give as much as they themselves have given.

Build your personal fundraising network by first identifying all of the groups with whom you and your organization interact and have meaningful relationships, such as personal friends, colleagues, relatives, vendors, elected officials, businesspeople. From each of these groups, identify one or two individuals who are especially well connected. Meet with them. Describe your program and fundraising goals, then find out if they are willing to assist you.

As soon as someone is willing to come on board, pow-wow with them privately. Find out who your new advocate thinks might be helpful to you. Learn everything you can, and plan a strategy for meeting with them. Don't hesitate to ask how much money your contact thinks others might be willing to give. Your circle of prospects—your network—will begin to grow immediately. Without a dynamic, personal network of interested people working on your behalf, your fundraising will not be successful.

A caveat: Maintain a professional relationship with the people who fundraise with you—even if you are close to them. As soon as you become too friendly and know them too well, you can lose your credibility and your objectivity. In all likelihood, you will back off from asking them for as much money or as much help as you should or as often as you should because your friendship with them will inhibit your doing so.

Resources

Michael Levine, *Selling Goodness: The Guerrilla P.R. Guide to Promoting Your Charity, Nonprofit Organization, or Fund-Raising Event*. Renaissance Books. Los Angeles, 1998.

Ruth Ellen Kinzey, *Using Public Relations Strategies to Promote Your Nonprofit Organization*. The Haworth Press. New York, 1999.

Applying This Principle to My Fundraising Success

List the names of five people who are likely to make contributions to your project.

_____

_____

_____

_____

_____

_____

_____

_____

_____

_____

List the names of five people who are likely to encourage others to make contributions.

_____

_____

_____

_____

_____

_____

_____

_____

_____

_____

List the names of five people who are likely to both give and get donations.

_____

_____

_____

_____

_____

_____

_____

_____

_____

_____

"She saw every personal relationship as a pair of intersecting circles."

– Jan Struther

Always Solicit Major Funds in Person

Fundraising is time-consuming and frustrating, particularly when you are trying to attract major gifts. To do things properly, you must research prospective donors, produce materials specifically for them, and find just the right people to assist you in approaching them.

Sometimes, in light of all of this preparatory work which may come to nothing, it is tempting to go for broke, to just write a letter on the off chance you will catch someone in the right mood on the right day. Resist all temptations to take short-cuts when soliciting major donors. In short order, you will earn a bad reputation among big donors, thereby undercutting your chances for future success.

You, or anyone else for that matter, will not receive large sums of money just because you write the most convincing letter. Don't think that you have a magic touch or some mystical amount of luck on your side. You don't.

Major gifts need to be solicited in person with materials highly personalized for each individual or entity and presented by someone who knows the person or organization being solicited.

Here are two useful tips for major funding solicitation.

→ First, find the right person to do the asking—someone to whom the potential donor cannot say, "No"—a respected philanthropist, a community leader. Most important, the right person would be someone who is a peer, someone who has given an amount equal to that being requested. In 99 out of 100 cases, you simply cannot ask a person who gives $100 to request $1 million.

The one exception to the peer-asking-a-peer formula may be a person who occupies a special place in your community; for example, a leading minority community leader who is known not to be wealthy but to be committed to improving the quality of life in underprivileged neighborhoods may be in a position to ask for a large sum of money. But even here, it would be preferable to have some big-money donor along to state the case and lend dollar-credibility to the cause.

→ Second, always outnumber the person being solicited. The ideal number is two people to make the case—someone who represents the program asking for the funds and the peer who does the actual asking.

Make certain that the people doing the asking complement each other appropriately and know their roles in the equation. The peer-asker, the one who has given substantial amounts of money, should always take the lead and glad-hand the prospective donor. Definitely, the staff or program person must take a back seat. He or she is there only to answer specific questions about the program's history, delivery, budget, other staff—all of the particulars about which you would expect anyone might reasonably ask.

Protocol dictates that you go to a donor before asking a donor to come to you. It is also good strategy. You want to get on your prospective donors' turf as quickly as you can, so you can size them up. Then, make every effort to get them to visit you as soon as possible. The sooner you are able to establish the bond, or emotional link, that may turn them into your supporter, the better.

Remember, when you become involved with major donors, they will become part of your personal and professional life. You will have a hard time drawing the line between where work and your private time begin and end. Be prepared to accept this part of being a successful fundraiser from the start or consider making a career change. You cannot raise major money half-heartedly by applying the brakes whenever it suits you.

You will know you have crossed the line between your professional and personal relationship with contributors if you give advice about how they should handle decisions in their lives or if you accept personal gifts from them. Always keep a safe distance or you risk losing a donor.

Resource

Barry J. McLeish, *The Donor Bond: How to Nurture Your Donors Using Strategic Marketing and Management Techniques.* Fund Raising Institute. Rockville, Maryland, 1991.

Applying This Principle to My Fundraising Success

Name at least five people who could make major contributions to your project, leaving two lines between each name.

_____

_____

_____

_____

_____

_____

_____

_____

_____

_____

_____

_____

_____

_____

_____

_____

_____

_____

_____

_____

_____

_____

Under each of their names add the name of at least one peer who should accompany the person from your staff making the solicitation.

_____

_____

_____

_____

_____

_____

*"We make a living by what we get. We make a life
by what we give."*

– Sir Winston Churchill

Go Where the Money Is Being Given Away

Some wise fundraiser once said, "You don't have to find the people who have the most money, but the people who are willing to give the most." Here are several tips that, if heeded, will aid in your success.

→ Look for people and organizations who already give.

Don't think that just because they have given, even in large amounts, they are tapped out. Their current level of giving may actually be just the tip of the iceberg. Go where the money is. Go where it's being given away.

→ Fundraising, other than the direct mail kind, is an extremely labor-intensive process.

Your time and resources are limited. So as soon as possible, you must narrow down the likeliest sources of major funding. You always want to find people whom others have overlooked but whom you can take the time to educate. Look for married couples in which one spouse is recognized for philanthropy, but the other stays in the shadows. You may be just the one to bring that person out. Look for the children of well-known philanthropists. They may have their own money (or access to their family's) and a desire to carry on the family tradition.

→ Some donors play games with fundraisers.

One game is playing hard to get. They know they can get attention from you if they intimate they have money to give. They also know how to withhold gifts, so they can remain the object of attention. At all times, be alert to being strung along.

→ Successful fundraisers develop their all-important, sixth sense which enables them to know where the money really is—and, just as important, where it is not.

They also relate to potential donors carefully and systematically, always testing the depth of their possible commitment. Develop subtle hoops (known only to you), through which people have to jump, so you can see the level of their interest, sincerity, and generosity.

→ Most charitable organizations print lists of their donors to acknowledge their levels of giving.

Begin to collect and make files of contributors, paying special attention to the names of people who appear more than once.

→ Go to where the money is.

If you want to solicit people for funds, you must get to know them personally. This means strategically placing yourself or your representative in organizations, on boards, or at social and professional events that will give you the opportunity to meet potential donors one-on-one.

→ Numerous publications profile individuals, corporations, and foundations that make substantial donations.

At first glance, these may appear to be all you will need. But beware, they are often out-of-date and inaccurate. In addition, they are available to everybody else. View them as a starting point and nothing more.

→ Learn to be a good listener.

People often say the opposite of what they really mean—or they may use words that mean one thing to you and quite another to them. When looking for sizable amounts of money, it may be wonderful to hear someone say, "I have always given and given and given money away"—until you find out that those gifts have never exceeded $25 each. You must be able tactfully to qualify someone's level of giving and willingness to give, or you will wind up stuck with donors who are nice people but not really able, or willing, to help you very much.

→ Get on your donors' turf as soon as possible.

Visit them in their office or at their home as soon as you can. Don't be impressed by lavishness or put off by meagerness. The richest people often downplay their wealth, while those with lesser resources often overplay them. You can learn valuable information about people's personality, history, and willingness to give from what they hang on their walls, the photographs they display, and the books they read.

→ Befriend accountants and lawyers.

You want to get people who know where the money is to work with you. If you can convince them of the value of your project, they can point you in the right direction without violating the confidentiality of their clients. Look for professionals who specialize in estates and trusts and in the dealings of large corporations. They know or should be able to find out the real financial picture of any individual, company, or foundation.

→ Know when to give up hope and cut your losses.

Learn to face reality. Heed the signs that someone is not willing or able to give to you, and extricate yourself politely; otherwise, you'll waste your limited time, energy, and money.

Resources

Annual Register of Grant Support
R.R. Bowker
121 Chanlon Road
New Providence, NJ 07974
(908) 464-6800

Joseph Dermer and Stephen Wertheimer, eds., *The Complete Guide to Corporate Fund Raising*. The Taft Group. Rockville, Maryland, 1982.

Applying This Principle to My Fundraising Success

Write the names of at least five corporations or foundations that could contribute to your project.

_____

_____

_____

_____

_____

List five accountants who might help you identify potential donors.

_____

_____

_____

_____

List five lawyers who specialize in wills and estates, who might work with you to find major donors.

_____

_____

_____

_____

"They take a paper and they read the headlines,
So they've heard of
unemployment and they've heard of
breadlines,
And they
philanthropically cure them all
By getting up a costume charity ball."

– Ogden Nash

Make Your Special Events Special

As you proceed in developing your project, you might find that one or more charitable, special events have a place in your over-all public relations and fundraising plan. They may be luncheons, dinners, gala events, theme parties, or other activities. They can turn out to be the best or the worst of times for you. It all depends on what you make of them. Make sure that you are in control of them, that they don't take on a life of their own, and that they re-inforce your fundraising purpose. Special events may or may not make you money, but they should never cost you money.

Following are eight tips for special events fundraising:

1. Don't put on an event just to put on an event.

   Be sure your event has a compelling reason for people to at-tend. For example, honoring someone who has contributed (either money or time, preferably both) to your cause. Make sure that the person you are honoring is well-respected and has some clout, so people will want to attend your event and make donations.

2. Be reasonable, not lavish.

   Avoid putting on events that are so extravagant that people might resent how their money is being spent. The event should not be about the food, the flowers, and the decorations. The focus should be on the cause, the progress you are making, and the needs you still have to fill.

3. Always aim for substantial underwriting, but not if it takes away major donations to your project or cause.

   It is sad but true that some people would sooner give $10,000 to underwrite the decorations for an event than make an out-right contribution to your worthy cause. Underwriting takes money directly away from your fundraising campaign and puts it in the hands of party planners and hotels. Try to influence contributors' priorities in favor of your cause. For example, suggest that a person willing to underwrite the $10,000 deco-rations give $7,500 for decorations and $2,500 directly to your organization and project. Surely, the decorations won't suffer, and your worthy cause will get cash it needs.

4. See the event as a means, not an end.

   That is, don't plan to make money on the event itself, but use it to meet people and cultivate relationships for your organization.

   This is an important distinction to observe. Your event should be budgeted at break-even. The revenue generated from ticket sales plus the monies you receive for underwriting should cover your costs. If you want to make money with the event, plan for premium or sponsored tables, an advertising journal, special donations in an honoree's name, or other similar ways to gen-erate additional revenue.

5. Beware of conflicts that arise between people putting on events. They can be your undoing.

You will need a core group of volunteers to make any special event successful. Unfortunately, they can end up fighting among themselves, jockeying for social position, and implicating or blaming you for what is not going smoothly—if you are not careful. From the start, recognize the high probability that you will be used as a scapegoat—so guard against being treated like one by keeping people focused on the goals of your fundraiser.

6. Make everyone feel special.

   At the event, make every attendee feel as though he or she is a million-dollar-donor, even if they are not. Wise fundraisers treat everyone alike because they know one can never be sure from whom or where major contributions are going to come.

7. Keep your eyes on the prize.

   In addition to obtaining some media exposure, the most important reason for staging your special event is to identify individuals who are potentially beneficial to your cause and to set the stage for developing ongoing relationships. One example of how to do this is to always make sure you have a professional photographer on hand. After the event, send copies of photographs to key people with the name of your organization prominently displayed on the mat of the picture. For those "special" individuals you wish to cultivate, consider professionally framing the photograph you send them. This may encourage them to display it on a desk or mantle for all to see.

8. Even when the event is over, it isn't over.

   In many ways, your after-event strategy is even more important than your initial planning. Always follow up with the people who attended. Capitalize on the goodwill you generated and smooth over any ruffled feathers. Keep people who attended involved in your organization as best you can; otherwise, you may have wasted a golden opportunity.

Resources

Susan J. Ellis, *From the Top Down: The Executive Role in Volunteer Program Success*. Revised Edition. Energize, Inc. Philadelphia, Pennsylvania, 1996.

Susan J. Ellis, *The Volunteer Recruitment Book*. Energize, Inc. Philadelphia, Pennsylvania, 1994.

Harry A. Freedman with Karen Feldman Smith, *Black Tie Optional: The Ultimate Guide to Planning and Producing Successful Special Events*. The Fund Raising Institute. Rockville, Maryland, 1991.

Flora MacLeod, *Motivating and Managing Today's Volunteers: How to Build and Lead a Terrific Team*. Self-Counsel Press. Bellingham, Washington, 1993.

Warrene Williams, *User Friendly Fund$Raising*. WorldComm. Alexander, North Carolina, 1994.

Applying This Principle to My Fundraising Success

List five ways to make everyone feel special at your special events.

_____

_____

_____

_____

_____

_____

_____

_____

_____

_____

*"The lamentable difficulty I have always experienced
[is] in saying 'no'."*

– Samuel Taylor Coleridge

Be Prepared to Look a Gift Horse in the Mouth

People give money in many different ways. In relatively few situations, do they make outright donations of large amounts of money without restrictions on how the money should be used. Unrestricted donations are the best gifts to obtain—and the hardest. More often, people give money for a specific purpose—constructing a building, establishing a scholarship fund, creating an animal shelter.

In some cases, people make pledges or give promises to pay their contribution out over a period of time. For example, a gift of $50,000 may be paid in two, or even five, installments. If that works for the donor and for you, that is fine. Others create trusts that go to charities before or after their deaths to offset estate taxes for the benefit of their heirs. Still others don't give money, but donate gifts-in-kind—a piano to a music program, ten computers to a high school computer laboratory, or a work of art to a museum.

The restrictions or lack of restrictions for any gift should be spelled out in writing and agreed to by you and your organization as well as the donor. All parties to the agreement should know exactly what is expected of them. Never take a verbal promise for any gift, especially if something is pledged over time. Hope for the best, but prepare for the worst. You must have legally binding documents to support your claims to a funder's contribution.

Do not give recognition for a gift until you have received the gift in full or until you have an unshakable agreement for receiving it.

You are in the business of fundraising. Naturally, you want to bring in gifts, but sometimes it costs you more to receive a gift than the gift may be worth to you. For example, the restrictions that a donor may place on a donation or the liabilities that may come with it may make it necessary for you to incur expenses that you would not have had otherwise. A gift of a collection of ancient coins to a historical museum may be interesting but impractical to receive because of prohibitive insurance costs. Sometimes, you must say, "No," even though you'd rather not.

Resist the temptation to talk about or formally publicize a gift until it has been signed, sealed, and delivered. It is only natural for you to want to shout about receiving a gift—particularly a major one. It did, after all, take a lot of your time and energy, and there were times you thought you might never get it. But don't make the potentially fatal mistake of rushing into publicity.

If you blather about a potential donation, you might offend donors who see premature publicity as a violation of the privacy of their dealings. In fact, they may never want their gift publicized—an unfortunate decision for you, perhaps, but one that is totally theirs to make. You could even lose an almost-closed gift to someone else who is able to snatch it out of your hands. Welcome to the cut-throat world of charitable solicitation.

Learn to keep your good news under wraps until gifts are closed, and you have discussed publicity with your donors—or you could be in for a rude awakening.

Resources

David G. Jacobs, ed., *The Foundation Directory 2003 Edition.* The Foundation Center. New York, 2003.

Pattie J. Johnson, ed., *Foundation Fundamentals: A Guide for Grantseekers.* Sixth Edition. The Foundation Center. New York, 1999.

Operating Grants for Nonprofit Organizations. Oryx Press. Phoenix, Arizona, 2000.

"Proposal Writing Short Course." The Foundation Center. New York. Available at *http://fdncenter.org/.*

Applying This Principle to My Fundraising Success

Make a list of at least five gifts-in-kind that you would be willing to accept.

_____

_____

_____

_____

_____

_____

_____

_____

_____

List at least five categories of restricted gifts for which you would want to raise money.

_____

_____

_____

_____

_____

_____

_____

_____

_____

_____

_____

_____

_____

_____

_____

_____

_____

_____

_____

_____

_____

_____

_____

_____

_____

_____

_____

"You can tell the character of every man when you see how he receives praise."

– Seneca

Create Your Donor Recognition Ladder

Some donors do not want to be publicly recognized for their gifts because they just don't want to become the target of other people's solicitations. You can hardly blame them. Some people go so far as to give anonymously. Whatever the case may be, the decision about publicity or recognition rests ultimately with donors. You must respect their wishes.

Most contributors are pleased to be honored. However, it is up to you to have a well-articulated recognition ladder in place, so potential donors know from the start what they can expect in the way of public acknowledgement. Your ladder can be a valuable marketing tool, especially in attracting the broadest possible spectrum of contributors.

Typically, a recognition ladder indicates progressive levels of giving and the name or title attached to each level of giving:

Grand benefactor: $75,000–99,999
Benefactor: $50,000–74,999
Major contributor: $25,000–49,999
Major donor: $10,000–24,999
Major sponsor: $5,000–9,999

Sometimes, the names assigned to giving levels reflect the mission or purpose of the project or organization receiving the funds. For example, if it is an historical organization, the levels could be something like founder, pioneer, pathfinder, and settler.

Along with each giving level, there should be a clear indication of what donors can expect for their gift. For example, gifts of certain amounts may be said to merit the name of the donor being inscribed on a wall in a prominent part of an appropriate building. Contributors of especially large gifts may have buildings, scholarships, or rooms named after them.

Consider gifts and plaques as a way of recognizing donors as well: gold or silver pins, indicating important giving levels; certificates of appreciation; and everything from coffee mugs to crystal vases. Acknowledgment of your appreciation for their support can help build bonds among you, your organization, and your donor base. Be sure to select recognition items that your donors can be proud to display. Your contributors' pride in showing off their affiliation with you will be the best kind of endorsement and public relations you and your organization can receive—the kind you cannot buy.

For the highest levels of giving, honor individuals with a title, membership in an exclusive giving club, or anything that sets them apart and brings them special recognition.

Most donors expect to be recognized. Neglect the courtesy of giving them their due at your own risk.

Resources

Mal Warick, *Raising Money By Mail: Strategies for Growth and Financial Stability*. Strathmoor Press. Berkeley, California, 1994–95.

Bohdan Romaniuk, project ed., *Corporate Giving Directory*, 25th Edition. The Taft Group. Farmington Hills, Michigan, 2003.

Applying This Principle to My Fundraising Success

Create a donor recognition ladder using categories that reflect the nature of your organization. For example, if your organization is a college, you might call some donors honorary alumni or *cum laude* contributors.

_____

_____

_____

_____

_____

_____

_____

_____

_____

_____

_____

_____

_____

_____

_____

_____

_____

_____

*"We cannot live only for ourselves.
A thousand fibers connect us with our
fellow men; and along those fibers, as
sympathetic threads, our actions run as causes, and
they come back to us as effects."*

– Herman Melville

Follow Up, Keep Track, and Look Back

Don't send your proposal off, thinking you are done with it. Submitting your proposal is only step one in a multi-step process of communication and cultivation—a process that almost never ends. Judicious follow-up is just as important as the overall concept of your project. You need to know how to keep in touch with a potential funding source without being over-anxious or obnoxious.

Don't think of rejection as a door's closing forever on your possibilities for funding. Look upon a "no" as a temporary setback or, perhaps, a detour. There are any number of reasons why you may have been turned down, none of which may have to do with the worthiness of your proposal. For example, every funding source has its own schedule, according to which it makes grants. Until

79

you get into the cycle of a funder's giving program, even a deserving project won't get funded. Eventually, you will learn how to juggle applying to several potential funders without going crazy.

Once you receive a donation, you must account for every penny of the gift. You have a legal obligation to keep scrupulous records of who gave what to you and how it was used. First of all, your records will provide your donors with important back-up tax information. Secondly, they will prove to your contributors that you have used their donation exactly as they directed it to be allocated.

Trust is essential to your successful long-term fundraising efforts. It takes years to build a meaningful relationship between an organization and its contributors, but that trust can be shattered in an instant, unless you pay attention to details and follow through. If the trust between you and a contributor is broken, it can seldom be reestablished. Make certain your records are impeccable, so you can never be successfully challenged on how you used contributed dollars.

In addition to providing necessary proof of how donated money was actually spent, you need accurate and detailed records to evaluate your fundraising program. Establish a useful computer database of donor prospects and active contributors, and keep it updated.

Ask anyone how much they want to raise for a given project, and their first answer is likely to be "as much as possible"; in other words, they have no realistic expectations. Consequently, they set up themselves and everyone else for defeat, because no matter how much money is raised, it will never seem to be enough. Keeping accurate records is the cornerstone of your information system. It allows you to analyze your data for information about patterns in giving to your organization, percentages of larger versus smaller gifts, and other trends that will enable you to learn from one fundraising cycle to another how to improve on your successes.

Write a formal, narrative report covering who gave, how much they gave, how they wanted the money used, and when the money came in. This report establishes several benchmarks (based on your own experience) you can use for increasing your success in future fundraising programs.

Think and act for the long-term when fundraising. These days, most of us are conditioned to pursue short-term goals and gain. However, in fundraising, the only thing that really matters is cultivating long-term relationships. As you build your donor base, you will be seeding the success of your future efforts.

Resources

Kent E. Dove, Jeffrey a. Lindauer, Carolyn P. Madvig, *Conducting A Successful Annual Giving Program: A Comprehensive Guide and Resource.* Jossey-Bass. San Francisco, California, 2001.

Christine Graham, *Keep the Money Coming: A Step-by-Step Guide to Annual Fundraising.* Revised Edition. Pineapple Press. Sarasota, Florida, 2001

Applying This Principle to My Fundraising Success

Create a hypothetical computer file that includes everything from the name, address, and e-mail to the giving history of every donor.

_____

_____

_____

_____

_____

_____

_____

_____

_____

"The purest treasure mortal times afford
Is spotless reputation."

– King Richard II, I, i, 177

Fortify Your Public Relations Approach

Credibility attracts money. Funders want to be assured that they are giving their support to an individual and organization that merits it. In part, they look upon their donation not just as a gift, but as an investment that is expected to produce results. They want to be certain that you and your organization represent a safe, long-term bet. So, it is your responsibility to create and maintain an impeccable image of yourself and your organization.

If you are a school, you want to be known as an institution that provides the highest quality education. Typically, you will stress the credentials of your faculty, the success of your graduates, and the resources of your campus(es). The same holds true if you are a hospital, a social service agency, or a research facility: accentuate the positive achievements of the people on your staff and the uniqueness of your facilities.

It is important to remember that building trust is an ongoing public relations strategy. A trustworthy image cannot be accomplished overnight or by you alone. Trust is developed over time, through the efforts of many people. Image-building must be looked upon as part of the standard operating procedure of your organization, -not as something necessary to the success of a single fundraising initiative. Obviously, public trust supports all of your efforts.

Today, everything good, bad, and indifferent competes for attention. In order to stand out from the crowd, you must create a strategy that puts the name of your organization and your collective successes before the public in the most positive light possible.

Good PR—PR that is positive, plentiful, and executed with foresight—is often easier talked about than accomplished. Therefore, you must be committed to an ongoing effort to generate positive press and general good feelings about your organization.

It is a fact that successful fundraisers understand the importance of implementing a focused, coordinated public relations strategy. They know that good PR is essential to attracting and maintaining a solid donor base and that those who dismiss PR as insubstantial hype, or who believe that good PR generates itself, are quite mistaken.

You may encounter resistance from those in your organization who don't understand the importance of good PR and may not be willing to allocate the time and resources necessary to achieve it. If this is the case, don't get bogged down in trying to defend your PR efforts against criticism. It can be difficult to prove that your PR has had a positive effect on your fundraising, especially early on. That kind of distraction will only keep you from moving forward. Plan for the inescapable constraints, set your strategy in motion, then follow it.

Remember that sometimes—in fact, more often than not—the cumulative results of your PR strategies may take years to come to fruition. Don't neglect them by focusing on short term gains because, eventually, they will pay off handsomely.

No matter how big or small your organization may be, your PR strategy should always have two focuses.

→ First, publicize the umbrella organization to which you and your project belong. Without establishing that credibility, your part cannot stand on its own. Your overall PR strategy should be all-encompassing and will entail developing a range of information: The history of the organization and its record of success—in short, all of the nonbudgetary elements of your case statement but reformatted for PR purposes.

→ Second, develop strategies to highlight the accomplishments of all the projects, programs, and units of your overall organization that are compatible with the PR focus you created for it.

Both PR focuses should reinforce each other. In the end, you will have developed a comprehensive campaign with many facets, all of which are interdependent.

Resources

Robert L. Dilenschneider, ed., *Dartnell's Public Relations Handbook*. Dartnell Corporation. Chicago, 1996.

Robert Davis, *It's The Little Things: Small Steps Toward Big Success in Public Relations*. Rutledge Books. Danbury, CT, 1998.

Applying This Principle to My Fundraising Success

How would you describe what your organization does in 25 words or less?

_____

_____

_____

_____

_____

What are your organization's goals?

_____

_____

_____

_____

_____

_____

_____

Do you have a mission statement. If so, what is it? If not, can you write one now?

_____

_____

_____

_____

_____

_____

_____

What are the three biggest successes your organization/project has had?

_____

_____

_____

_____

What do you want your target audience to believe/know/understand about your organization/project?

_____

_____

_____

_____

_____

*"Except ye utter by the tongue words easy to under-
stand, how shall it be known what is spoken?"*

– First Corinthians 14:9

Plan a Comprehensive Public Relations Campaign

Now that you've had a chance to think about your PR strategy in general, it's time to focus on the specifics. Your PR strategy is really a person-to-person effort to get out positive information about you, your project, and your organization. Once you have defined whom you want to reach and what your messages are, you can begin to identify the ways in which you will reach them—your communications channels.

In some circumstances, your ongoing PR campaign may involve a completely different group of people from those directly involved in your fundraising efforts; in others, they may overlap. Often, those you cultivate for PR purposes will not be the same people you cultivate for contributions, even though their efforts on your behalf will be crucial to your fundraising success. Knowing which people to cultivate for which purpose is another important key to your PR strategy.

Other important keys to keep in mind while building your PR strategy include the following:

→ Define your message. Create your theme.

You need a catchy, but substantive, phrase to describe and position your organization and/or project. You must have, as political satirist Tom Lehrer once said, "a tune that the people can hum." In some cases, this is called a "mission statement." If your mission statement is too long, which is often the case, you might want to turn into a slogan. The United Way, for example, has and uses both. Its mission statement reads "The mission of United Way is to improve people's lives by mobilizing the caring power of communities"; its current slogan or catch phrase is "The Way America Cares. Community by Community." While the mission statement needs to remain consistent over time, slogans may be altered and updated to fit the current program or project; such is the case with the United Way.

It's important to refrain from tooting one's horn or sounding self-serving. Instead, create an outer-directed message that will resonate with other people and startle them into appreciating all the good you do and can continue to do with their support. The United Way's message is a good example to follow.

→ Establish a budget for PR.

For those who think that PR means "free publicity," the reality may come as a shock. At the very least, you must plan for costs connected with designing and printing materials, the possibility of hiring a PR professional to write and disseminate information to the media, and staging special events. While you may be able to defray some of these costs through sponsorships, underwriting, and volunteers, you don't want to count on them when preparing your budget. Though some in your organization or on the board of directors may balk at these expenditures, underscore their importance and be ready to defend them when presenting your budget.

→ Identify your existing audiences, the ones that already know you, and determine ways to reach them with your message.

Make a list of all of the different constituencies with whom you regularly interact, and indicate how you typically reach them: through a newsletter or e-mail, by personal letter or phone. Come up with at least one new way to communicate with them. Typically, people are assaulted with so many messages in the media, that they begin to tune out even those things that appeal to and interest them—including yours. In order to remain fresh in people's thinking, you have to come up with new vehicles through which you can reach them. They will pay extra attention when they see a reference to you in a new place, and your credibility will increase. One form of media reinforces another: Just the fact that news and information about you appears in a new and different venue will increase their respect for you.

→ Target new audiences.

Don't become old news. You must constantly be identifying new audiences to reach with your message. Obviously, you need to target as many new people as you can in as cost-effective a way as possible, but don't overlook the power of finding large, new constituencies through one-on-one introductions. Large associations and groups are always led by small groups of influential people. Meet with them individually and enlist their support in reaching their group's membership. You will save tons of money; and you'll be able to get a unique feel for the broader audience, so you can tailor an effective message to them.

→ Enlist and educate influential spokespersons, including experts, who can potentially speak on behalf of your project.

You don't need celebrities to take up your cause, although they can be highly effective when the right ones come along. However, you do need well-placed community leaders to be ambassadors for you. Leaders tend to move through many groups of people. As they carry word about you to the public-at-large and to influential special interest groups, they will invariably pick up information of use to you.

→ Develop professionally written, visual, and other materials you will need to get your message out.

Find a professional to create your communications materials and be prepared to spend some—not necessarily a great deal of—money. Don't make the mistake of trying to do everything yourself. Even though you may be able to write, chances are you are not the best person to write your brochure or to find or create the right visuals for your communications package. Developing such materials takes special talent and abilities. In addition, the person doing it should be able to be objective about your organization and programs. You are probably too close to what you do to know what kind of wording and visuals will resonate with outside audiences.

→ Set dates for special events.

You need an ongoing (monthly, bi-monthly, quarterly) series of programs that will keep your name before the public and involve people in your organization. Don't be afraid to set dates and stick with them. Give yourself time for your audience(s) to build.

→ Prepare an ongoing, two-year PR timetable that is updated and extended by one year each year. Because it takes time to build good PR, you must have a long-term perspective.

→ Create assessment tools or benchmarks to measure the success of your PR efforts.

Resources

Merr Aronsom & Don Spetner, *The Public Relations Writer's Handbook*. Lexington Books. Jossey-Bass. San Francisco, 1993.

Philip Lesly, ed., *Lesly's Public Relations Handbook*. Third Edition. Prentice-Hall. Englewood Cliffs, NY, 1983.

Irene M. Lober, *Promoting Your School: A Public Relations Handbook*. Technomic Publishing. Lancaster, PA, 1993.

Applying This Principle to My Fundraising Success

Who is/are your primary target audience(s)?

_____

_____

_____

_____

_____

What are their ages, socio-economic level(s), and other pertinent information?

_____

_____

_____

_____

_____

_____

List five spokespersons who might speak on behalf of your project.

_____

_____

_____

_____

Identify the major media outlets in your city, state, and region.

_____

_____

_____

_____

_____

"Someone said of nations—but it might well have been said of individuals, too—that they require 'something sufficiently akin to be understood, something sufficiently different to provoke attention, and something sufficiently great to command admiration.'"

– Phoebe Low

Develop Different Approaches for the Different Media

Anyone who wants to be successful must become media savvy—something that's easier said than done.

Dealing with the media can be a challenging and sometimes frustrating experience, particularly if you are new to it. For the most part, journalists are wary of PR people, believing that there is always an agenda hidden between the lines of the press release you or your PR person send out. And, honestly, they are right. By sending out news about your organization you are looking for publicity that will in some way benefit your fundraising efforts. They know that and you know that, so now the question is, How do you get them to print or otherwise disseminate your information in spite of your "hidden agenda"?

The best way to work successfully with the media is to construct different messages and different approaches for each medium. Too often we forget that we adjust our thinking and speaking when addressing different individuals and audiences. For example, if you are a sophisticated researcher in an esoteric medical field, you would speak with a colleague quite differently than you would with someone who has a general interest in what you are studying but no in-depth knowledge of your specialization. It is no different when you are communicating with the media. Each medium is different. Each has its pluses and minuses in terms of getting your message across. So, you must package the information you send to each of them differently.

If you are the individual in your organization responsible for working directly with the media, it is important that you make an effort to appeal to the self-interest of each medium—their need to attract readers, viewers, or listeners. One way is to give them grabbers (verbal and visual attention getters). Put yourself in their shoes. It is difficult for them to wow a jaded public, so be sure to present stories in a form they can easily use.

Here are some other ways to work with the media to your mutual benefit:

→ Approach newspapers with longer, more thoughtful press releases or story ideas on hot topics for the general reader. The print media can devote substantial space to in-depth feature coverage.

→ Send op-ed pieces and letters-to-the-editor as a way of promoting your cause without paying to do so. If you're not the expert or wish to remain behind the scene, find either someone in your organization or an influential donor to pen the op-ed piece or letter (with your guidance, of course).

→ Approach magazines with articles for specialized audiences—musicians, doctors, lawyers, teachers—that are typically more interested and knowledgeable about the subject than the average newspaper reader.

→ Television reporters and producers tend to think in visual terms. Provide them with story ideas that not only have strong visuals but that also tug at the emotions of viewers. An example would be a young cancer survivor leaving the hospital and thanking the American Cancer Society for its help.

→ Approach talk radio programs to do in-depth interviews. Most talk radio hosts like topics that are current and that will elicit reaction—hopefully positive in your case—from their listeners.

→ If you are the head of your organization, never designate or allow a PR person to run interference between you and reporters. That will only anger and frustrate media professionals who are trying to do their job. The last thing you want to do is alienate the media. If you are your organization's PR person, facilitate open media access (when appropriate) to your director(s). This will go a long way toward getting you the media coverage you desire.

→ Produce and distribute an experts list describing the specialties of professionals in your organization and their availability to the media. Provide phone numbers at which people are willing to be contacted by the media. Highlight the topics on which they are qualified to speak described in terms that the different media will find enticing (e.g., visual for TV people, topical for a talk radio host). You will be amazed at how appreciative the media will be. A cautionary note: Be certain that your experts are available, articulate, and media savvy.

Update your list regularly, perhaps quarterly. Disseminate your experts list beyond your local area. You can gain national attention by distributing it widely or including it on your Web site.

Media people come and go. Never assume that, once you've established contacts, your work is done. You must constantly renew your media relationships.

Applying This Principle to My Fundraising Success

In one sentence, describe a publicity-worthy subject which you think would interest the media in your fundraising project.

_____

_____

_____

_____

_____

Briefly write up the idea so that it will appeal to a newspaper, which can cover it in depth; a radio talk show that would capitalize on the controversy surrounding it; and a TV news program that would want to capture its emotional/visual appeal.

_____

_____

_____

_____

_____

_____

_____

_____

_____

List all the experts within your organization whom the media might contact about the subject, and how they wish to be reached.

_____

_____

_____

_____

_____

"What we have done for ourselves alone dies with us. What we have done for others and the world remains and is immortal."

– Albert Pine

Lavish Recognition on Your Donors

Nothing is what it seems. When asked, most people will say that they don't really want to be recognized for their contributions, that the joy of giving is enough. Don't make the mistake of taking such modesty at face value. They are simply telling you what they think is expected of a generous person.

Acknowledgement is part of the pleasure of being a donor—to be identified as someone special. Proceed on the assumption that it is up to you to take the initiative in donor recognition, to show people how much you care. Do not put them in the demeaning position of lobbying on their own behalf.

As logical and polite as it should be to recognize contributors, unfortunately, too many fundraisers do a bad job of it and, therefore, wind up doing the unthinkable—turning a friend into an enemy.

They undo all the goodwill they have worked so hard to create with a contributor, once the donation has been received.

Perhaps, such miscalculation is the natural by-product of the obsessive pursuit of the next best gift. Blinded by the need to generate more and bigger dollars, people lose sight of how important it is to appreciate and recognize past or recent supporters.

If you want to succeed in the long term, recognizing past donors must be a cornerstone of your fundraising and public relations strategies. Appreciation of those who help you achieve your goals will repay itself again and again in ever-increasing dollars contributed.

Ultimately, donor recognition benefits you. Everybody loves a winner. Nobody wants to be on a losing team. If you publicize the contributions that previous and current donors have made to your success, you send important signals to the general public and to people who may be interested in giving to your effort.

Eventually the general public will become aware of your program and the success you are having. Potential donors will see that you treat contributors well and will have the assurance that they can give to a cause that already has support.

Of course, the simplest way for you to recognize donors is to send out press releases highlighting their support, but you want to do much more than that. You might consider holding a donor recognition luncheon, dinner, or reception—something that brings all of your contributors together at one time in one place, so you can put them in the limelight. You will want to recognize those who have made contributions at different levels in different ways.

If you have been fortunate enough to attract major donations, you might consider honoring one individual each year by holding a testimonial event. Such a program could turn into an additional opportunity to raise funds, but it should not be orchestrated with that as the focus.

The primary purpose should be recognition for past generosity. What comes as a result of that—and much will accrue to your benefit—is icing on the cake.

Resource

Melba Beals, *Expose Yourself: Using the Power of Public Relations to Promote Your Business and Yourself.* Chronicle Books. San Francisco, 1990.

Applying This Principle to My Fundraising Success

Describe at least five creative ways to recognize your donors.

_____

_____

_____

_____

_____

_____

_____

_____

_____

_____

_____

_____

_____

_____

_____

_____

_____

_____

*"You are rich enough to give small amounts of
money to worthy causes when you can buy all the
groceries you need."*

– Sharon K. Yntema

Publicize How Contributions Are Being Used

Publicity is not worth anything unless it motivates people to contribute to your organization, even if the message is subtle. Good publicity has the same aim as good advertising: to get other people to do something. Your publicity should be as strategically conceived as anything else in your overall fundraising campaign.

Take nothing for granted. Always assume that nobody knows anything about you, even though they might. No matter how much publicity you may receive, no matter how many times people within your organization and circle of professional and personal friends tell you how wonderful your project is, proceed as though nobody ever heard of you. You must constantly generate information that reinforces the idea that giving to your organization is the best thing that anyone can do.

101

Along with recognizing donors, publicizing the positive effects of charitable contributions should be a mainstay of your public relations strategy. Contributions should be looked upon as investments and publicized as such.

When you approach potential donors, stress the fact that, as with any business venture, the money they donate will generate positive returns. Of course, they won't be financial returns—no one will make a profit from their donation. But the people who will be served by your organization—such as through improved health care, education, or the arts—and society-at-large will receive a direct benefit. That will be the pay off.

Identify individuals whose lives have been improved through your efforts, funded by contributions, and get them to speak on behalf of your program. Their participation in your public relations efforts can often create a sense of drama and importance, which in turn can evoke an emotional response. Don't be afraid of tugging at the heartstrings of potential donors, because emotion, or passion, is the underpinning of all successful fundraising.

Including an interview with a student who has benefited from receiving a scholarship in your newsletter or in a human interest press release are perfect examples of how to humanize the positive effect of donation—particularly if that individual has a compelling, say "rags-to-riches," story. A well written and well placed article about someone who benefits so directly and dramatically from your organization's efforts, can often serve to inspire multiple donors to come forward.

Remain alert to the power that visual images have to communicate a message. Whenever possible, include a photograph and a descriptive caption that illustrates the positive effect of a particular contribution with your press release.

Most of all, be fresh, timely, and compelling when you contact the media. Readers, viewers, and listeners, as well as journalists, quickly recognize and shun organizations that waste their time with unimportant and inconsequential information. Your public relations efforts should subtly, or even dramatically, set other contributions in motion, thus creating a domino effect that will directly benefit your cause.

Resource

Kathleen A. Neal, *A Primer on Nonprofit PR.* Pineapple Press, Inc. Sarasota, Florida, 2001.

Applying This Principle to My Fundraising Success

List three very different people whose lives have been positively affected by programs or services you offer.

_____

_____

_____

_____

_____

_____

In 25 words or less, tell each person's story. Focus on who they were, what circumstances they were in, how your organization helped them, and what charitable contributions enabled you to provide the assistance you gave them.

_____

_____

_____

_____

_____

_____

"To do anything in this world worth doing, we must not stand back shivering and thinking of the cold and danger, but jump in, and scramble through as well as we can."

– Sydney Smith

Spread Good News Via Your Donor Network

There is no way around the fact that fundraising can be a laborious activity. Major gifts cannot be solicited successfully by machine or through direct mail. People must be cultivated over time. You need a large cadre of ambassadors to spread the word about your cause.

It is best not to think of cultivating your ambassadors for the purpose of getting an immediate gift, although it's always a possibility. Instead, look upon it as an ongoing process that will repay itself down the line. Be prepared to spend a great deal of time, energy, and even money to make money. In fundraising, as in business, you must commit and spend development resources in order to reap benefits.

There are those givers—generous or not—who want to limit their involvement to writing checks to one cause or another. They've met their obligation once they've made their donation. Others— the most valuable people in your donor network—are not only givers, they are doers. They can be enlisted to take the ball and run with it. They will spread the word about the value of your organization and its fundraising efforts, thereby becoming your best ambassadors. In addition, these same people will probably give more to you from their own funds as time goes on. As they "sell" others on the value of your program, they often "sell" themselves on giving even more.

With a bit of time and effort, you can actually transform some "givers" into "doers" through a combination of training, educating, and sometimes pampering. It is important to help your givers fully understand that, as valuable as their donations are to your cause, their willingness to promote your cause to others by helping with fundraising activities, even when they don't fundraise directly, is of equal value. Such encouragement can often attract and retain the most valuable donor an organization can have—a giver who does.

Your best ambassadors will demonstrate certain characteristics and have other behaviors in common:

→ Look for contributors who are outgoing and who are not afraid to promote themselves and your cause.

Some people simply have a flair for publicity; they know how to present themselves in public and draw constructive attention to what they are doing. Learn to recognize such individuals early on and then capitalize on their charisma.

→ Look for donors who are active in their community—those who belong to different professional and business associations.

Their business contacts can be of great value, and an association's weekly/monthly/annual meetings offer opportunities to talk about your organization or project. If you are particularly fortunate, you may even gain access to one or more mailing lists of groups to which your donors belong—an invaluable addition to your fundraising tool kit.

→ Look for supporters who are social.

Without being pushy, ask them to invite you to private parties to which you otherwise might not have entree. Informal associations will mean everything to you, as will the credibility of your appearing in exclusive settings and situations.

Resource

Kay Sprindel Grace and Alan L. Wendroff, *High Impact Philanthropy: How Donors, Boards, and Nonprofit Organizations Can Transform Communities.* John Wiley & Sons. New York, 2001.

Applying This Principle to My Fundraising Success

List at least three extroverted ambassadors for your organization, who might already have donated or who are likely to do so.

_____

_____

_____

_____

Identify ways—meetings, social events, entree to important individuals—they might open doors for you.

_____

_____

_____

_____

_____

_____

_____

Contact your potential ambassadors and, if they agree to help,
develop a strategy with them for spreading good news about
your project.

"Baby, what a big surprise,
Right before my very eyes."

– Peter Cetera

Inform Your Colleagues of Your Fundraising Efforts

Someone once advised that the three most important things to consider in buying a piece of real estate are location, location, and location. In fundraising, the three may be said to be communication, communication, and communication.

Yet, people typically make the mistake of thinking that communications tools have to be slick and elaborate and that the audiences they want to reach are only external to their organization. Too often, people in your position overlook the obvious—all of the potential that is around them.

Working in an organization, big or small, one is usually surrounded by people who have the power to be the first line of support.

Secretaries, receptionists, professional colleagues in other departments, a host of people with whom you may come in contact—all of these coworkers can be powerful advocates, assisting you in disseminating positive information about your fundraising project. They can be links to all kinds of organizations and individuals you might never have thought of or been able to reach. Don't make the regrettable error of typecasting people by the job in which they work. Discount no one because of often-misleading circumstantial cues.

Use every opportunity to inform those closest to you about the initiation and progress of your fundraising projects. Make them feel as though they are part of your team, even if they are not directly involved in the fundraising part of your project or organization. The more an individual feels included in the process, the more likely he or she is to spread the word.

Consider producing an internal newsletter. It doesn't have to be elaborate or necessarily include pictures or extensive graphics. Even a brief, typewritten update on fundraising activities can go a long way toward building internal goodwill and making your colleagues feel as though they are involved. When they feel involved, they will generally be supportive.

Another simple method for reaching your internal audience is to invite your colleagues to periodic brown bag luncheons, where you can discuss your fundraising progress in a casual atmosphere. You supply the food, of course. In all of this, however, there are two important caveats of which you should be aware:

> First, people have a natural tendency to be wary of becoming involved with the unknown. Try your best to seek out those people who are likely to be genuinely supportive of your efforts from the beginning. Provide them with enough information so they can, in turn, pass on that information to those who might be somewhat negative to begin with. The more information that is available, the less skeptical people will be of your efforts.

Second, remember that, even when you go about informing your internal audiences about your fundraising, you should not talk about sensitive matters that might violate potential donors' privacy. Only provide details of gifts that have been closed, and then only if you have the permission of the donors. Talk in vague generalities about gifts in the works. Never reveal the names of potential contributors until the check has cleared and you are certain they don't mind being identified.

On balance, it will be to your advantage to take as much of the mystery out of fundraising as you can within your organization. And one of the best ways to accomplish this is to reach out to those with whom you interact daily.

Resources

Gregory R. Sherwin & Emily N. Avila, *Connecting Online: Creating a Successful Image on the Internet.* The Oasis Press. Grants Pass, Oregon, 1997.

Shel Holtz, *Public Relations on the Net: Winning Strategies to Inform and Influence the Media, the Investment Community, the Government, the Public, and More!* American Management Association. New York, 1999.

Applying This Principle to My Fundraising Success

List at least five ways you can keep people within your organization informed of your fundraising plans—and successes.

_____

_____

_____

_____

_____

Identify as many people as you can within your organization who would be most helpful to you.

_____

_____

_____

_____

_____

_____

_____

_____

_____

Write a strategy for your internal communications program, including a timetable for implementation.

_____

_____

_____

_____

_____

_____

_____

_____

_____

_____

_____

_____

_____

_____

"Two roads diverged in a wood, and I—
I took the one less traveled by,
And that has made all the difference."

– Robert Frost

Establish a Meaningful Internet Presence

Being on the Internet is standard operating procedure for most organizations. It will be a fact of our lives until it is replaced by telepathy or whatever the next frontier of communication may be. Yet, few have realized how to use the Internet effectively for direct fundraising. It is the Gold Rush of the 21st century, in which everyone has pitched a tent, but few have been able to strike it rich. The promise of success looms for every savvy fundraiser, if you follow a few simple steps.

Most Web sites are simply single-dimension brochures transplanted digitally from the printed page into cyberspace. Material that sat uninspired in formal publications now shows up equally blandly on computer screens, where it probably has to be scrolled—to the frustration of its readers. Not only does there have to be a better way, there is one.

Here are some common sense tips for turning your Web site into a meaningful vehicle that can support your fundraising.

→ You must go beyond just being on the Web.

Give people a reason for regularly returning to your Web site. Consider creating a dynamic news and information site, to which people may refer often for the latest information in fields related to your organization.

If you are in health care, rather than just talking about your programs and institution, why not create a news and information section which will provide useful material to professionals and the general public—a series of timely bulletins generated by your researchers and clinicians? Make part of your Web site free information, another part a subscription service to generate revenue.

→ Actively promote your Web site in every possible venue.

Many good sites languish because no one knows they even exist. Use your newsletters, other publications, and even advertising to interest people in your site.

→ Keep your Web site updated.

You cannot publish a Web site and then forget about it. In an age of instant communication, there is nothing more discouraging than seeing an out-of-date Web site. Appoint an Internet czar; someone needs to have the responsibility for keeping your site fresh and interesting. If you can't find one, learn how to update your site yourself. Unless that task is made one person's job, and taken seriously, it will never be done properly.

→ Link your Web site to every other possible site so that you spread the word about your programs and fundraising efforts.

→ Tailor your content to search engines; otherwise, you are less likely to be found.

→ Encourage people to e-mail you and experts within your organization, then respond to them quickly and personally. In today's world people expect instant response. Give it to them.

→ Establish a consultant service, through which people can pay for personalized advice that they receive from your experts.

→ Create a way for people to make contributions to your nonprofit using their credit cards. In addition to promoting the ongoing needs of your organization, spotlight a Program-of-the-Month or special initiative that needs resources.

→ Raise money on the Internet by offering coffee mugs, men's ties, women's scarves, calendars—a warehouse of souvenirs from your organization.

Transform your nonprofit's Web site into a fundraising tool. Over time, you'll generate major money.

Resources

Gary B. Grant, Gary B. Grobman, and Steve Roller, *The Wilder Nonprofit Field Guide to Fundraising on the Internet*. Amherst H. Wilder Foundation. St. Paul, Minnesota, 1999.

Michael Johnston, *Direct Response Fund Raising: Mastering New Trends for Results*. John Wiley & Sons. New York, 2001.

Applying This Principle to My Fundraising Success

Jot down five ways you can make your Web site more interactive.

_____

_____

_____

_____

_____

_____

Explore five ways you can raise money for your organization using the Internet.

_____

_____

_____

_____

_____

_____

_____

_____

_____

_____

_____

_____

_____

_____

_____

_____

_____

_____

_____

_____

_____

_____

_____

_____

_____

_____

"One is the loneliest number that you'll ever do."

– Three Dog Night

Remember that the Buck Stops with You

Fundraising is often done by committee; the most successful fundraising, however, is not. The best fundraisers are usually lone rangers—fiercely independent, close-mouthed, and driven when it comes to achieving their goals. Typically, they're poor team-players and seldom share their resources and tactics. They invest large amounts of personal energy in establishing person-to-person relationships, knowing these relationships cannot simply be turned over to someone else. They prefer to operate unfettered by organizational bureaucracy. Ultimately, you will have to balance your need for flexibility, freedom, and independence with the practical necessity of empowering others to assist you—without your losing control.

When working in an organization, it is important to establish a network of other people to ensure your fundraising success. You must work through other people. You must detach and delegate responsibility for advancing the purposes of your fundraising. You must be prepared to let others run with the ball. You must praise others and downplay even justifiable kudos directed at you. In other words, you must be a leader rather than a lone wolf.

To be effective and successful in fundraising, you must be tactful and subtile when working with others. For example, you must be able to stay in control of the people with whom you work (especially volunteers), without their feeling the heavy hand of authoritarianism or manipulation. Also, you must applaud their efforts and support their need to feel of value to you and the organization. The real art of fundraising management is the ability to guide and motivate others to achieve their and your organization's mutual goals. Otherwise, you will loose their cooperation.

If you are your organization's primary spokesperson, it will fall upon you to interact with and handle media relations. This is a task that should not be delegated to volunteers or people outside the organization. Some larger fundraising projects or organizations will have at least one public relations/media relations professional on staff, so your control of and interactions with this individual will depend on your role in the organization.

Assuming the task of media relations falls solely on your shoulders, ultimately everything about promoting the fundraising for your project will depend upon your ability to handle the media. You may look and look for surrogates, but no one can take your place. The need for good media relations will outlast any specific project or event. Never take a back seat in dealing with the press.

If you consider yourself shy or retiring, or are not by nature a joiner, you're going to find fundraising a difficult and uncomfortable task. To be a successful fundraiser, you will have to meet, greet, and schmooze with individuals and groups alike. You will have to become involved in organizations and activities that will help get your message out. As long as you are committed to seeking funding, you will never again enjoy the luxury of being reticent or retiring. You may often have to give up evenings, weekends, even holidays.

It is your enthusiasm, commitment, and passion—as well as the nature of your cause—that will ultimately inspire and motivate everyone with whom you work to identify and acquire funding. You must be willing to set an example, so you can't afford to be passive.

There is no escape. The burden is squarely on you. And that's good because the cause in which you believe so passionately receives the benefits of all the good will and giving that accrues from your tireless efforts. And that's your reward.

Resource

Ronald R. Jordan and Katelyn L. Quynn, *Planned Giving for Small Nonprofits*. John Wiley & Sons. New York, 2002.

Applying This Principle to My Fundraising Success

Describe five ways you can work constructively with others while retaining control over your fundraising program.

_____

_____

_____

_____

_____

_____

_____

_____

"Success depends on three things: who says it, what he says, and how he says it; and of these three things, what he says is the least important."

– John, Viscount Morley

Heed the Unwritten Rule

The old truism, "It isn't what you know but who you know," counts more, perhaps, than we would like it to. And fundraising is no exception. To be successful, you must establish your own power base.

If you look upon fundraising as simply a professional endeavor, if you do everything recommended from Days 1 through 29, but neglect the advice in Day 30, you will not succeed. On the other hand, if you follow the advice in Day 30, but ignore everything in Days 1 through 29, you might not only get your foot in the door in the short run, you could even succeed long-term.

You can dot every "i" and cross every "t," but your assiduousness won't count for much unless you master the political aspects of fundraising.

Identify the power people within your organization, community, or sphere of contacts—those individuals who make the determinant decisions that affect you and your cause.

One method for maximizing your contacts and power resources is called the "Rule of Nine." Take an inventory of all your existing contacts, either inside or outside your organization, who can make a difference in your fundraising efforts. Spend your initial time and effort meeting with those individuals who can help you reach at least nine other influential people. Meet with those individuals first, then move on to contacts with less "know who." You may find that of those nine, two or more may know another nine influential people and so on. With this method, you can soon build up an extensive contact list of potentially powerful donors.

Remember, too, that the ability to donate large sums of money is not necessarily the only criterion for identifying someone as an influential contact. There are invariably those in your community who are important to include in your list of contacts because they are in policy- and decision-making positions. Not all fundraising projects need these sorts of individuals on board, but it is always wise to seek them out.

An important part of the politics of your fundraising is making certain that people appreciate the value and effectiveness of your efforts. Too often, even successful people are reluctant to document their own accomplishments. Don't be afraid, for example, to circulate data on, say, the cost-effectiveness of your fundraising activities or to compare your expenses with those of other fundraisers by obtaining national or local information. Individuals in positions of political or financial power sometimes react better to a factual, even statistical, approach than to a tug on the emotional heartstrings. In general, providing a little of each is the wisest course.

Like everything in life, fundraising is a game. It has its written and unwritten rules. Winners know how to play by both. People will try to make you jump higher and higher through hoops. To be successful, you have to be willing to go through the paces and still land squarely on your feet. Ignore the politics of your efforts at your own peril.

Resources

The Foundation Center, *Promoting Issues and Ideas: A Guide to Public Relations for Nonprofit Organizations*, 2nd Edition. M. Booth & Associates, Inc. 1995.

Sondra C. Shaw and Martha A. Taylor, *Reinventing Fundraising: Realizing the Potential of Women in Fundraising.* Jossey-Bass Publishers. San Francisco, California, 1995.

Applying This Principle to My Fundraising Success

List at least five power people who really make the decisions that affect you and your cause, and how you can keep them on your side.

_____

_____

_____

_____

_____

List ten donors who can help you get to nine other donors.

_____

_____

_____

_____

_____

_____

_____

_____

_____

_____

List ten people who may not give your organization money, but who may help you reach others who might.

_____

_____

_____

_____

_____

_____

_____

_____

_____

_____

Establish a simple, yet ongoing, way you will demonstrate the effectiveness of your efforts, without appearing as though you're just blowing your own horn.

_____

_____

_____

_____

_____

_____

_____

_____

_____

_____

_____

_____

"Ideas go booming through the world louder than cannon. Thoughts are mightier than armies. Principles have achieved more victories than horsemen or chariots."

– W. M. Paxton

Mastering Your Program

Day 31, after you finish *30 Days to Successful Fundraising*, is the first day of the rest of your fundraising life. As always, it is up to you to use it most profitably.

The question that you may have asked yourself from Day 1 is, "What happens after 30 days?" Here's what I suggest.

Take a few days and review, day by day, each of the 30 days. Reread the notes you took on achieving each success principle. Jot down where you think you are in achieving and applying the principles. Rate yourself high, medium, or low—and describe why you rate yourself that way. Then, based upon the results of your self-assessment, identify—in order, one day at a time—those days you feel still need work. Pay most attention to the concepts and information about which you feel somewhat unsure.

Once you feel you have a solid understanding of the concepts and principles set forth in this book, you will be ready to design, develop, and implement a successful and personally rewarding fundraising campaign. And remember, *30 Days to Successful Fundraising* is intended to be your program. Its greatest value will be in your personalizing and adapting it to your ongoing needs. Good luck and good fundraising!

Applying This Principle to My Fundraising Success

Starting with Day 1, rate yourself high, medium, or low in applying the fundraising success principles.

Day 1	Day 16
Day 2	Day 17
Day 3	Day 18
Day 4	Day 19
Day 5	Day 20
Day 6	Day 21
Day 7	Day 22
Day 8	Day 23
Day 9	Day 24
Day 10	Day 25
Day 11	Day 26
Day 12	Day 27
Day 13	Day 28
Day 14	Day 29
Day 15	Day 30

Review the days you feel you still need to work on.

Repeat the process until you feel you have mastered all 30 days.

About the Author

Author, television personality, columnist, and consultant to non-profit and for-profit organizations, Dr. Stephen L. Goldstein is president and CEO of Educational Marketing Services, Inc., a company he founded in 1977. He is a nationally recognized marketing, communications, and fundraising executive, as well as a trends analyst and forecaster. The EMS Network of Consulting Professionals provides expertise in fundraising, communications, marketing, advertising, and market research, analysis and strategy that enhances the success and organizational effectiveness of government agencies, non-profit organizations, public policy institutes, professional associations, and for-profit businesses.

Dr. Goldstein earned his bachelor's, master's, and Ph.D. from Columbia University. He is the author of *You Can't Go Wrong by Doing It Right: 50 Principles for Running A Successful Business,* published by PSI Research in March 1999. Stephen Goldstein is also a widely published contributor of articles on subjects ranging from education and politics to the economy and trends. His columns have appeared in *The Los Angeles Times*, *Newsday*, *The Miami Herald*, *The Chicago Sun-Times*, and other leading national and international publications. Currently, he writes a bi-weekly editorial column for *The Sun-Sentinel* (Ft. Lauderdale, Florida). His columns have been translated into Spanish and published in *Vision*.

Dr. Goldstein is the producer and host of "We the People," a half-hour, general interest and public affairs television interview program, which is broadcast by Comcast Communications seven days a week. He also hosts "Teen Talk," produced by BECON television. From 1998 through 2001, Dr. Goldstein was the executive producer and host of "The Business Exchange," a regional, half-hour, weekly television program produced and broadcast by WLRN, public television in South Florida.

Group Book Sales and Seminars

You can save money by ordering copies of *30 Days to Successful Fundraising* in bulk at (800) 228-2275. Better yet, get the book "live." You can schedule Dr. Goldstein for a seminar tailored to your group's special needs, on site at your location. You'll benefit from training all of your staff at the same time. If your organization is small, you can invite professionals and volunteers from other non-profits to join your seminar; everyone will benefit—most of all you. To schedule a seminar, call (954) 772-4455.